BY BERTRAND RUSSELL

NEW HOPES FOR A CHANGING WORLD
UNPOPULAR ESSAYS
AUTHORITY AND THE INDIVIDUAL
HUMAN KNOWLEDGE: ITS SCOPE AND LIMITS
HISTORY OF WESTERN PHILOSOPHY

BERTRAND RUSSELL

THE
IMPACT OF SCIENCE
ON
SOCIETY

SIMON AND SCHUSTER

NEW YORK

1953

80610
6-53

PREFATORY NOTE

This book is based upon lectures originally given at Ruskin College, Oxford, England. Three of these—Chapter I, "Science and Tradition," Chapter II, "General Effects of Scientific Techniques," and Chapter VI, "Science and Values"—were subsequently repeated at Columbia University, New York, and published by the Columbia University Press. None of the other chapters have been published before in the United States. The last chapter in the present book, "Can a Scientific Society be Stable?" was the Lloyd Roberts Lecture given at the Royal Society of Medicine, London.

CONTENTS

CHAPTER I

Science and Tradition

MAN has existed for about a million years. He has possessed writing for about 6,000 years, agriculture somewhat longer, but perhaps not much longer. Science, as a dominant factor in determining the beliefs of educated men, has existed for about 300 years; as a source of economic technique, for about 150 years. In this brief period it has proved itself an incredibly powerful revolutionary force. When we consider how recently it has risen to power, we find ourselves forced to believe that we are at the very beginning of its work in transforming human life. What its future effects will be is a matter of conjecture, but possibly a study of its effects hitherto may make the conjecture a little less hazardous.

The effects of science are of various very different kinds. There are direct intellectual effects: the dispelling of many traditional beliefs, and the adoption of others suggested by the success of scientific method. Then there are effects on technique in industry and war. Then, chiefly as a consequence of new techniques, there are profound changes in social organization which are gradually bringing about corresponding political changes. Finally, as a result of the new control over the environment which scientific knowledge has conferred, a new philosophy is growing up, involving a changed conception of man's place in the universe.

I shall deal successively with these aspects of the effects of science on human life. First I shall recount its purely intellectual effect as a solvent of unfounded traditional beliefs, such as witchcraft. Next, I shall consider scientific technique, especially since the industrial revolution. Last, I shall set forth the philosophy which is being suggested by the triumphs of science, and shall contend that this philosophy, if unchecked, may inspire a form of unwisdom from which disastrous consequences may result.

The study of anthropology has made us vividly aware of the mass of unfounded beliefs that influence the lives of uncivilized human beings. Illness is attributed to sorcery, failure of crops to angry gods or malignant demons. Human sacrifice is thought to promote victory in war and the fertility of the soil; eclipses and comets are held to presage disaster. The life of the savage is hemmed in by taboos, and the consequences of infringing a taboo are thought to be frightful.

Some parts of this primitive outlook died out early in the regions in which civilization began. There are traces of human sacrifice in the Old Testament, for instance in the stories of Jephthah's daughter and of Abraham and Isaac, but by the time the Jews became fully historical they had abandoned the practice. The Greeks abandoned it in about the seventh century B.C. But the Carthaginians still practiced it during the Punic Wars. The decay of human sacrifice in Mediterranean countries is not attributable to science, but presumably to humanitarian feelings. In other respects, however, science has been the chief agent in dispelling primitive superstitions.

Eclipses were the earliest natural phenomena to escape

from superstition into science. The Babylonians could predict them, though as regards solar eclipses their predictions were not always right. But the priests kept this knowledge to themselves, and used it as a means of increasing their hold over the populace. When the Greeks learned what the Babylonians had to teach, they very quickly arrived at astonishing astronomical discoveries. Thucydides mentions an eclipse of the sun, and says that it occurred at the new moon, which, he goes on to observe, is apparently the only time at which such a phenomenon can occur. The Pythagoreans, very shortly after this time, discovered the correct theory of both solar and lunar eclipses, and inferred that the earth is a sphere from the shape of its shadow on the moon.

Although, for the best minds, eclipses were thus brought within the domain of science, it was a long time before this knowledge was generally accepted. Milton could still speak of times when the sun

> In dim eclipse, disastrous twilight sheds
> On half the nations, and with fear of change
> Perplexes monarchs.

But in Milton this had become only poetic license.

It was very much longer before comets were brought within the compass of science; indeed the process was completed only by the work of Newton and his friend Halley. Caesar's death was foretold by a comet; as Shakespeare makes Calpurnia say:

> When beggars die, there are no comets seen;
> The heavens themselves blaze forth the death of princes.

The Venerable Bede asserted: "comets portend revolutions of kingdoms, pestilence, war, winds, or heat." John

Knox regarded comets as evidence of divine anger, and his followers thought them "a warning to the King to extirpate the Papists." Probably Shakespeare still held beliefs of a superstitious kind about comets. It was only when they were found to obey the law of gravitation, and when some at least were found to have calculable orbits, that educated men in general ceased to regard them as portents.

It was in the time of Charles II that scientific rejection of traditional superstitions became common among educated men. Charles II perceived that science could be an ally against the "fanatics," as those who regretted Cromwell were called. He founded the Royal Society, and made science fashionable. Enlightenment spread gradually downwards from the Court. The House of Commons was as yet by no means as modern in outlook as the King. After the plague and the Great Fire, a House of Commons Committee inquired into the causes of those misfortunes, which were generally attributed to divine displeasure, though it was not clear to what the displeasure was due. The Committee decided that what most displeased the Lord was the works of Mr. Thomas Hobbes. It was decreed that no work of his should be published in England. This measure proved effective: there has never since been a plague or a Great Fire in London. But Charles, who liked Hobbes because Hobbes had taught him mathematics, was annoyed. He, however, was not thought by Parliament to be on intimate terms with Providence.

It was at this time that belief in witchcraft began to be viewed as a superstition. James I was a fanatical persecutor of witches. Shakespeare's *Macbeth* was a piece of government propaganda, and no doubt the witches in that play made it more acceptable as a piece of flattery of the monarch. Even

Bacon pretended to believe in witchcraft, and made no protest when a Parliament of which he was a member passed a law increasing the severity of the punishment of witches. The climax was reached under the Commonwealth, for it was especially Puritans who believed in the power of Satan. It was partly for this reason that Charles II's government, while not yet venturing to deny the possibility of witchcraft, was much less zealous in searching it out than its predecessors had been. The last witchcraft trial in England was in 1664, when Sir Thomas Browne was a witness against the witch. The laws against it gradually fell into abeyance, and were repealed in 1736—though, as late as 1768, John Wesley continued to support the old superstition. In Scotland the superstition lingered longer: the last conviction was in 1722.

The victory of humanity and common sense in this matter was almost entirely due to the spread of the scientific outlook—not to any definite argument, but to the impossibility of the whole way of thinking that had been natural before the age of rationalism that began in the time of Charles II, partly, it must be confessed, as a revolt against a too rigid moral code

Scientific medicine had, at first, to combat superstitions similar to those that inspired belief in witchcraft. When Vesalius first practiced dissection of corpses, the Church was horrified. He was saved from persecution, for a time, by the Emperor Charles V, who was a valetudinarian, and believed that no other physician could keep him in health. But after the Emperor died, Vesalius was accused of cutting people up before they were dead. He was ordered, as a penance, to go on a pilgrimage to the Holy Land; he was shipwrecked, and died of exposure. In spite of his work and that of Hervey and other great men, medicine continued to be largely superstitious. Insanity, in particular, was thought to be due to possession by evil spirits, and was therefore treated by subjecting the insane to cruelties which it was hoped the demons would dislike. George III, when mad, was still treated on this principle. The ignorance of the general public continued even longer. An aunt of mine, when her husband quarreled with the War Office, was afraid that the worry would cause him to develop typhus. It is hardly till the time of Lister and Pasteur that medicine can be said to have become scientific. The diminution of human suffering owing to the advances in medicine is beyond all calculation.

Out of the work of the great men of the seventeenth century a new outlook on the world was developed, and it was this outlook, not specific arguments, which brought about the decay of the belief in portents, witchcraft, demoniacal possession, and so forth. I think there were three ingredients in the scientific outlook of the eighteenth century that were specially important:

(1) Statements of fact should be based on observation, not on unsupported authority.
(2) The inanimate world is a self-acting, self-perpetuating system, in which all changes conform to natural laws.
(3) The earth is not the center of the universe, and probably Man is not its purpose (if any); moreover, "purpose" is a concept which is scientifically useless.

These items make up what is called the "mechanistic outlook," which clergymen denounce. It led to the cessation of persecution and to a generally humane attitude. It is now less accepted than it was, and persecution has revived. To those who regard its effects as morally pernicious, I commend attention to these facts.

Something must be said about each of the above ingredients of the mechanistic outlook.

(1) *Observation versus Authority:* To modern educated people, it seems obvious that matters of fact are to be ascertained by observation, not by consulting ancient authorities. But this is an entirely modern conception, which hardly existed before the seventeenth century. Aristotle maintained that women have fewer teeth than men; although he was twice married, it never occurred to him to verify this statement by examining his wives' mouths. He said also that children will be healthier if conceived when the wind is in the north. One gathers that the two Mrs. Aristotles both had to run out and look at the weathercock every evening before going to bed. He states that a man bitten by a mad dog will not go mad, but any other animal will (*Hist. An.* 704a); that the bite of the shrewmouse is dangerous to horses, especially if the mouse is pregnant (ibid., 604b); that elephants suffering from insomnia can be cured by rubbing their shoulders with salt, olive oil, and warm water (ibid., 605a); and so on and so on. Nevertheless, classical dons, who have never observed any animal except the cat and the dog, continue to praise Aristotle for his fidelity to observation.

The conquest of the East by Alexander caused an immense influx of superstition into the Hellenistic world. This was particularly notable as regards astrology, which almost all later pagans believed in. The Church condemned it, not on scientific grounds, but because it implied subjection to Fate. There is, however, in St. Augustine, a scientific argument against astrology quoted from one of the rare pagan skeptics.

The argument is that twins often have very different careers, which they ought not to have if astrology were true.

At the time of the Renaissance, belief in astrology became a mark of the free thinker: it must be true, he thought, because the Church condemned it. Free thinkers were not yet any more scientific than their opponents in the matter of appeal to observable facts.

Most of us still believe many things that in fact have no basis except in the assertions of the ancients. I was always told that ostriches eat nails, and, though I wondered how they found them in the Bush, it did not occur to me to doubt the story. At last I discovered that it comes from Pliny, and has no truth whatever.

Some things are believed because people feel as if they *must* be true, and in such cases an immense weight of evidence is necessary to dispel the belief. Maternal impressions are a case in point. It is supposed that any notable impression on the mother during gestation will affect the offspring. This notion has scriptural warrant: you will remember how Jacob secured speckled kine. If you ask any woman who is not a scientist or an associate of scientists, she will overwhelm you with incidents in proof of the superstition. Why, there was Mrs. So-and-So, who saw a fox caught in a trap, and sure enough her child was born with a fox's foot. Did you know Mrs. So-and-So? No, but my friend Mrs. Such-and-Such did. So, if you are persistent, you ask Mrs. Such-and-Such, who says: "Oh no, *I* didn't know Mrs. So-and-So, but Mrs. What's-Her-Name did." You may spend a lifetime in the pursuit of Mrs. So-and-So, but you will never catch up with her. She is a myth.

The same situation occurs in regard to the inheritance of acquired characters. There is such a strong impulse to believe in this that biologists have the greatest difficulty in persuading people of the contrary. In Russia they have failed to convince Stalin, and have been compelled to give up being scientific in this matter.

When Galileo's telescope revealed Jupiter's moons, the orthodox refused to look through it, because they knew there could not be such bodies, and therefore the telescope must be deceptive.

Respect for observation as opposed to tradition is difficult and (one might almost say) contrary to human nature. Science insists upon it, and this insistence was the source of the most desperate battles between science and authority. There are still a great many respects in which the lesson has not been learned. Few people can be convinced that an obnoxious habit—e.g. exhibitionism—cannot be cured by punishment. It is pleasant to punish those who shock us, and we do not like to admit that indulgence in this pleasure is not always socially desirable.

(2) *The autonomy of the physical world:* Perhaps the most powerful solvent of the pre-scientific outlook has been the first law of motion, which the world owes to Galileo, though to some extent he was anticipated by Leonardo da Vinci. The first law of motion says that a body which is moving will go on moving in the same direction with the same velocity until something stops it. Before Galileo it had been thought that a lifeless body will not move of itself, and if it is in motion it will gradually come to rest. Only living beings, it was thought, could move without help of some external agency. Aristotle thought that the heavenly bodies were pushed by gods. Here on earth, animals can set themselves in motion and can cause motion in dead matter. There are, it was conceded, certain kinds of motion which are "natural"

to dead matter: earth and water naturally move downwards, air and fire upwards; but beyond these simple "natural" motions everything depends upon impulsion from the souls of living beings.

So long as this view prevailed, physics as an independent science was impossible, since the physical world was thought to be not causally self-contained. But Galileo and Newton between them proved that all the movements of the planets, and of dead matter on the earth, proceed according to the laws of physics, and once started, will continue indefinitely. There is no need of mind in this process. Newton still thought that a Creator was necessary to get the process going, but that after that He left it to work according to its own laws.

Descartes held that not only dead matter, but the bodies of animals also, are wholly governed by the laws of physics. Probably only theology restrained him from saying the same of human bodies. In the eighteenth century French free thinkers took this further step. In their view, the relation of mind and matter was the antithesis of what Aristotle and the scholastics had supposed. For Aristotle, first causes were always mental, as when an engine driver starts a freight train moving and the impulsion communicates itself from truck to truck. Eighteenth-century materialists, on the contrary, considered all causes material, and thought of mental occurrences as inoperative by-products.

(3) *The dethronement of "purpose"*: Aristotle maintained that causes are of four kinds; modern science admits only one of the four. Two of Aristotle's four need not concern us; the two that do concern us are the "efficient" and the "final" cause. The "efficient" cause is what we should call simply "the cause"; the "final" cause is the purpose. In human affairs this distinction has validity. Suppose you find a restau-

rant at the top of a mountain. The "efficient" cause is the carrying up of the materials and the arranging of them in the pattern of a house. The "final" cause is to satisfy the hunger and thirst of tourists. In human affairs, the question "why?" is more naturally answered, as a rule, by assigning the final cause than by setting out the efficient cause. If you ask "why is there a restaurant here?" the natural answer is "because many hungry and thirsty people come this way." But the answer by final cause is only appropriate where human volitions are involved. If you ask "why do many people die of cancer?" you will get no clear answer, but the answer you want is one assigning the efficient cause.

This ambiguity in the word "why" led Aristotle to his distinction of efficient and final causes. He thought—and many people still think—that both kinds are to be found everywhere: whatever exists may be explained, on the one hand, by the antecedent events that have produced it, and, on the other hand, by the purpose that it serves. But although it is still open to the philosopher or theologian to hold that everything has a "purpose," it has been found that "purpose" is not a useful concept when we are in search of scientific laws. We are told in the Bible that the moon was made to give light by night. But men of science, however pious, do not regard this as a scientific explanation of the origin of the moon. Or, to revert to the question about cancer, a man of science may believe, in his private capacity, that cancer is sent as a punishment for our sins, but *qua* man of science he must ignore this point of view. We know of "purpose" in human affairs, and we may suppose that there are cosmic purposes, but in science it is the past that determines the future, not the future the past. "Final" causes, therefore, do not occur in the scientific account of the world.

In this connection Darwin's work was decisive. What

Galileo and Newton had done for astronomy, Darwin did for biology. The adaptations of animals and plants to their environments were a favorite theme of pious naturalists in the eighteenth and early nineteenth centuries. These adaptations were explained by the Divine Purpose. It is true that the explanation was sometimes a little odd. If rabbits were theologians, they might think the exquisite adaptation of weasels to the killing of rabbits hardly a matter for thankfulness. And there was a conspiracy of silence about the tapeworm. Nevertheless, it was difficult, before Darwin, to explain the adaptation of living things to their environment otherwise than by means of the Creator's purposes.

It was not the fact of evolution, but the Darwinian mechanism of the struggle for existence and the survival of the fittest, that made it possible to explain adaptation without bringing in "purpose." Random variation and *natural* selection use only *efficient* causes. This is why many men who accept the general fact of evolution do not accept Darwin's view as to how it comes about. Samuel Butler, Bergson, Shaw, and Lysenko will not accept the dethronement of purpose—though in the case of Lysenko it is not God's purpose, but Stalin's, that governs heredity in winter wheat.

(4) *Man's place in the universe:* The effect of science upon our view of man's place in the universe has been of two opposite kinds; it has at once degraded and exalted him. It has degraded him from the standpoint of contemplation, and exalted him from that of action. The latter effect has gradually come to outweigh the former, but both have been important. I will begin with the contemplative effect.

To get this effect with its full impact, you should read simultaneously Dante's *Divine Comedy* and Hubble on the *Realm of the Nebulae*—in each case with active imagination and with full receptiveness to the cosmos that they portray. In Dante, the earth is the center of the universe; there are ten concentric spheres, all revolving about the earth; the wicked, after death, are punished at the center of the earth; the comparatively virtuous are purged on the Mount of Purgatory at the antipodes of Jerusalem; the good, when purged, enjoy eternal bliss in one or other of the spheres, according to the degree of their merit. The universe is tidy and small: Dante visits all the spheres in the course of twenty-four hours. Everything is contrived in relation to man: to punish sin and reward virtue. There are no mysteries, no abysses, no secrets; the whole thing is like a child's doll's house, with people as the dolls. But although the people were dolls they were important because they interested the Owner of the doll's house.

The modern universe is a very different sort of place. Since the victory of the Copernican system we have known that the earth is not the center of the universe. For a time the sun replaced it, but then it turned out that the sun is by no means a monarch among stars, in fact, is scarcely even middle class. There is an incredible amount of empty space in the universe. The distance from the sun to the nearest star is about 4·2 light years, or 25×10^{12} miles. This is in spite of the fact that we live in an exceptionally crowded part of the universe, namely the Milky Way, which is an assemblage of about 300,000 million stars. This assemblage is one of an immense number of similar assemblages; about 30 million are known, but presumably better telescopes would show more. The average distance from one assemblage to the next is about 2 million light years. But apparently they still feel they haven't elbow room, for they are all hurrying away from each other; some are moving away from us at the rate of

14,000 miles a second or more. The most distant of them so far observed are believed to be at a distance from us of about 500 million light years, so that what we see is what they were 500 million years ago. And as to mass: the sun weighs about 2×10^{27} tons, the Milky Way about 160,000 million times as much as the sun, and is one of a collection of galaxies of which about 30 million are known. It is not easy to maintain a belief in one's own cosmic importance in view of such overwhelming statistics.

So much for the contemplative aspect of man's place in a scientific cosmos. I come now to the practical aspect.

To the practical man, the nebulae are a matter of indifference. He can understand astronomers' thinking about them, because they are paid to, but there is no reason why *he* should worry about anything so unimportant. What matters to him about the world is what he can make of it. And scientific man can make vastly more of the world than unscientific man could.

In the pre-scientific world, power was God's. There was not much that man could do even in the most favorable circumstances, and the circumstances were liable to become unfavorable if men incurred the divine displeasure. This showed itself in earthquakes, pestilences, famines, and defeats in war. Since such events are frequent, it was obviously very easy to incur divine displeasure. Judging by the analogy of earthly monarchs, men decided that the thing most displeasing to the Deity is a lack of humility. If you wished to slip through life without disaster, you must be meek; you must be aware of your defenselessness, and constantly ready to confess it. But the God before whom you humbled yourself was conceived in the likeness of man, so that the universe seemed human and warm and cozy, like home if you are the youngest of a large family, painful at times, but never alien and incomprehensible.

In the scientific world, all this is different. It is not by prayer and humility that you cause things to go as you wish, but by acquiring a knowledge of natural laws. The power you acquire in this way is much greater and much more reliable that that formerly supposed to be acquired by prayer, because you never could tell whether your prayer would be favorably heard in heaven. The power of prayer, moreover, had recognized limits; it would have been impious to ask too much. But the power of science has no known limits. We were told that faith could remove mountains, but no one believed it; we are now told that the atomic bomb can remove mountains, and everyone believes it.

It is true that if we ever did stop to think about the cosmos we might find it uncomfortable. The sun may grow cold or blow up; the earth may lose its atmosphere and become uninhabitable. Life is a brief, small, and transitory phenomenon in an obscure corner, not at all the sort of thing that one would make a fuss about if one were not personally concerned. But it is monkish and futile—so scientific man will say—to dwell on such cold and unpractical thoughts. Let us get on with the job of fertilizing the desert, melting Arctic ice, and killing each other with perpetually improving technique. Some of our activities will do good, some harm, but all alike will show our power. And so, in this godless universe, we shall become gods.

Darwinism has had many effects upon man's outlook on life and the world, in addition to the extrusion of purpose of which I have already spoken. The absence of any sharp line between men and apes is very awkward for theology. When did men get souls? Was the Missing Link capable of sin and therefore worthy of hell? Did Pithecanthropus Erectus have moral responsibility? Was Homo Pekiniensis damned? Did Piltdown Man go to heaven? Any answer must be arbitrary.

But Darwinism—especially when crudely misinterpreted —threatened not only theological orthodoxy but also the creed of eighteenth-century liberalism. Condorcet was a typical liberal philosopher of the eighteenth century; Malthus developed his theory to refute Condorcet; and Darwin's theory was suggested by Malthus's. Eighteenth-century liberals had a conception of man as absolute, in its way, as that of the theologians. There were the "Rights of Man"; all men were equal; if one showed more ability than another, that was due entirely to a better education, as James Mill told his son to prevent him from becoming conceited.

We must ask again: Should Pithecanthropus, if still alive, enjoy "The Rights of Man"? Would Homo Pekiniensis have been the equal of Newton if he could have gone to Cambridge? Was the Piltdown Man just as intelligent as the present inhabitants of that Sussex village? If you answer all all these questions in the democratic sense, you can be pushed back to the anthropoid apes, and if you stick to your guns, you can be driven back ultimately on to the amoeba, which is absurd (to quote Euclid). You must therefore admit that men are not all congenitally equal, and that evolution proceeds by selecting favorable variations. You must admit that heredity has a part in producing a good adult, and that education is not the only factor to be considered. If men are to be conventionally equal politically, it must be not because they are really equal biologically, but for some more specifically political reason. Such reflections have endangered political liberalism, though not, to my mind, justly.

The admission that men are not all equal in congenital

endowment becomes dangerous when some group is singled
out as superior or inferior. If you say that the rich are abler
than the poor, or men than women, or white men than black
men, or Germans than men of any other nation, you proclaim
a doctrine which has no support in Darwinism, and which is
almost certain to lead to either slavery or war. But such
doctrines, however unwarrantable, have been proclaimed in
the name of Darwinism. So has the ruthless theory that the
weakest should be left to go to the wall, since this is Nature's
method of progress. If it is by the struggle for existence that
the race is improved—so say the devotees of this creed—let
us welcome wars, the more destructive the better. And so we
come back to Heraclitus, the first of fascists, who said:
"Homer was wrong in saying 'would that strife might
perish from among gods and men.' He did not see that he was
praying for the destruction of the universe. . . . War is
common to all, and strife is justice. . . . War is the father
of all and king of all; and some he has made gods and some
men, some bond and some free."

It would be odd if the last effect of science were to revive a
philosophy dating from 500 B.C. This was to some extent
true of Nietzsche and of the Nazis, but it is not true of any
of the groups now powerful in the world. What *is* true is that
science has immensely increased the sense of human power.
But this effect is more closely connected with science as
technique than with science as philosophy. In this chapter I
have tried to confine myself to science as a philosophy,
leaving science as technique for later chapters. After we have
have considered science as technique I shall return to the
philosophy of human power that it has seemed to suggest. I
cannot accept this philosophy, which I believe to be very
dangerous. But of that I will not speak yet.

CHAPTER II

General Effects of
Scientific Technique

SCIENCE, ever since the time of the Arabs, has had two functions: (1) to enable us to *know* things, and (2) to enable us to *do* things. The Greeks, with the exception of Archimedes, were only interested in the first of these. They had much curiosity about the world, but, since civilized people lived comfortably on slave labor, they had no interest in technique. Interest in the practical uses of science came first through superstition and magic. The Arabs wished to discover the philosopher's stone, the elixir of life, and how to transmute base metals into gold. In pursuing investigations having these purposes, they discovered many facts in chemistry, but they did not arrive at any valid and important general laws, and their technique remained elementary.

However, in the late Middle Ages two discoveries were made which had a profound importance: they were gunpowder and the mariner's compass. It is not known who made these discoveries—the only thing certain is that it was *not* Roger Bacon.

The main importance of gunpowder, at first, was that it

enabled central governments to subdue rebellious barons. Magna Carta would have never been won if John had possessed artillery. But although in this instance we may side with the barons against the king, in general the Middle Ages suffered from anarchy, and what was needed was a way of establishing order and respect for law. At that time, only royal power could achieve this. The barons had depended upon their castles, which could not stand against guns. That is why the Tudors were more powerful than earlier kings. And the same kind of change occurred at the same time in France and Spain. The modern power of the State began in the late fifteenth century and began as a result of gunpowder. From that day to this, the authority of States has increased, and throughout it has been mainly improvement in weapons of war that has made the increase possible. This development was begun by Henry VII, Louis XI, and Ferdinand and Isabella. It was artillery that enabled them to succeed.

The mariner's compass was equally important. It made possible the age of discovery. The New World was opened to white colonists; the route to the East round Cape of Good Hope made possible the conquest of India, and brought about important contacts between Europe and China. The importance of sea power was enormously increased, and through sea power Western Europe came to dominate the world. It is only in the present century that this domination has come to an end.

Nothing of equal importance occurred in the way of new scientific technique until the age of steam and the industrial revolution. The atom bomb has caused many people during the last seven years to think that scientific technique may be carried too far. But there is nothing new in this. The industrial revolution caused unspeakable misery both in England

and in America. I do not think any student of economic history can doubt that the average of happiness in England in the early nineteenth century was lower than it had been a hundred years earlier; and this was due almost entirely to scientific technique.

Let us consider cotton, which was the most important example of early industrialization. In the Lancashire cotton mills (from which Marx and Engels derived their livelihood), children worked from twelve to sixteen hours a day; they often began working at the age of six or seven. Children had to be beaten to keep them from falling asleep while at work; in spite of this, many failed to keep awake and rolled into the machinery, by which they were mutilated or killed. Parents had to submit to the infliction of these atrocities upon their children, because they themselves were in a desperate plight. Handicraftsmen had been thrown out of work by the machines; rural laborers were compelled to migrate to the towns by the Enclosure Acts, which used Parliament to make landowners richer by making peasants destitute; trade unions were illegal until 1824; the government employed *agents provocateurs* to try to get revolutionary sentiments out of wage-earners, who were then deported or hanged.

Such was the first effect of machinery in England.

Meanwhile the effects in the United States had been equally disastrous.

At the time of the War of Independence, and for some years after its close, the Southern States were quite willing to contemplate the abolition of slavery in the near future. Slavery in the North and West was abolished by a unanimous vote in 1787, and Jefferson, not without reason, hoped to see it abolished in the South. But in the year 1793 Whitney invented the cotton gin, which enabled a Negro to clean fifty pounds of fiber a day instead of only one, as formerly. "Laborsaving" devices in England had caused children to have to work fifteen hours a day; "laborsaving" devices in America inflicted upon slaves a life of toil far more severe than what they had to endure before Mr. Whitney's invention. The slave trade having been abolished in 1808, the immense increase in the cultivation of cotton after that date had to be made possible by importing Negroes from the less southerly States in which cotton could not be grown. The deep South was unhealthy, and the slaves on the cotton plantations were cruelly overworked. The less Southern slave States thus became breeding-grounds for the profitable Southern graveyards. A peculiarly revolting aspect of the traffic was that a white man who owned female slaves could beget children by them, who were his slaves, and whom, when he needed cash, he could sell to the plantations, to become (in all likelihood) victims of hookworm, malaria, or yellow fever.

The ultimate outcome was the Civil War, which would almost certainly not have occurred if the cotton industry had remained unscientific.

There were also results in other continents. Cotton goods could find a market in India and Africa; this was a stimulus to British imperialism. Africans had to be taught that nudity is wicked; this was done very cheaply by missionaries. In addition to cotton goods we exported tuberculosis and syphilis, but for them there was no charge.

I have dwelt upon the case of cotton because I want to emphasize that evils due to a new scientific technique are no new thing. The evils I have been speaking of ceased in time: child labor was abolished in England, slavery was abolished in America, imperialism is now at an end in India. The evils that persist in Africa have now nothing to do with cotton.

Steam, which was one of the most important elements in the industrial revolution, had its most distinctive sphere of operation in transport—steamers and railways. The really large-scale effects of steam transportation did not develop fully till after the middle of the nineteenth century, when they led to the opening of the Middle West of America and the use of its grain to feed the industrial populations of England and New England. This led to a very general increase of prosperity, and had more to do than any other single cause with Victorian optimism. It made possible a very rapid increase in population in every civilized country —except France, where the Code Napoléon had prevented it by decreeing equal division of a man's property among all his children, and where a majority were peasant proprietors owning very little land.

This development was not attended with the evils of early industrialism, chiefly, I think, because of the abolition of slavery and the growth of democracy. Irish peasants and Russian serfs, who were not self-governing, continued to suffer. Cotton operatives would have continued to suffer if English landowners had been strong enough to defeat Cobden and Bright.

The next important stage in the development of scientific technique is connected with electricity and oil and the internal-combustion engine.

Long before the use of electricity as a source of power, it was used in the telegraph. This had two important consequences: first, messages could now travel faster than human beings; secondly, in large organizations detailed control from a center became much more possible than it had formerly been.

The fact that messages could travel faster than human beings was useful, above all, to the police. Before the telegraph, a highwayman on a galloping horse could escape to a place where his crime had not yet been heard of, and this made it very much harder to catch him. Unfortunately, however, the men whom the police wish to catch are frequently benefactors of mankind. If the telegraph had existed, Polycrates would have caught Pythagoras, the Athenian government would have caught Anaxagoras, the Pope would have caught William of Occam, and Pitt would have caught Tom Paine when he fled to France in 1792. A large proportion of the best Germans and Russians have suffered under Hitler and Stalin; many more would have escaped but for the rapid transmission of messages. The increased power of the police therefore, is not wholly a gain.

Increase of central control is an even more important consequence of the telegraph. In ancient empires satraps or proconsuls in distant provinces could rebel, and had time to entrench themselves before the central government knew of their disaffection. When Constantine proclaimed himself Emperor at York and marched on Rome, he was almost under the walls of the city before the Roman authorities knew he was coming. Perhaps if the telegraph had existed in those days the Western world would not now be Christian. In the War of 1812, the battle of New Orleans was fought after peace had been concluded, but neither army was aware of the fact. Before the telegraph, ambassadors had an independence which they have now completely lost, because they had to be allowed a free hand if swift action was necessary in a crisis.

It was not only in relation to government, but wherever organizations covering large areas were concerned, that the telegraph effected a transformation. Read, for instance, in Hakluyt's *Voyages*, the accounts of attempts to foster trade with Russia that were made by English commercial interests in the time of Elizabeth. All that could be done was to choose an energetic and tactful emissary, give him letters, goods, money, and leave him to make what headway he could. Contact with his employers was possible only at long intervals, and their instructions could never be up to date.

The effect of the telegraph was to increase the power of the central government and diminish the initiative of distant subordinates. This applied not only to the State, but to every geographically extensive organization. We shall find that a great deal of scientific technique has a similar effect. The result is that fewer men have executive power, but those few have more power than such men had formerly.

In all these respects, broadcasting has completed what the telegraph began.

Electricity as a source of power is much more recent than the telegraph, and has not yet had all the effects of which it is capable. As an influence on social organization its most notable feature is the importance of power stations, which inevitably promote centralization. The philosophers of Laputa could reduce a rebellious dependency to submission by interposing their floating island between the rebels and the sun. Something very analogous can be done by those who control power stations, as soon as a community has become dependent upon them for lighting and heating and cooking. I lived in America in a farmhouse which depended entirely upon electricity, and sometimes, in a blizzard, the wires would be blown down. The resulting inconvenience was almost intolerable. If we had been deliberately cut off for being rebels, we should soon have had to give in.

The importance of oil and the internal-combustion engine in our present technique is obvious to everybody. For technical reasons, it is advantageous if oil companies are very large, since otherwise they cannot afford such things as long pipe lines. The importance of oil companies in the politics of the last thirty years has been very generally recognized. This applies especially to the Middle East and Indonesia. Oil is a serious source of friction between the West and the U.S.S.R., and tends to generate friendliness towards communism in some regions that are strategically important to the West.

But what is of most importance in this connection is the development of flying. Airplanes have increased immeasurably the power of governments. No rebellion can hope to succeed unless it is favored by at least a portion of the air force. Not only has air warfare increased the power of governments, but it has increased the disproportion between great and small Powers. Only great Powers can afford a large air force, and no small Power can stand out against a great Power which has secure air supremacy.

This brings me to the most recent technical application of physical knowledge—I mean the utilization of atomic energy. It is not yet possible to estimate its peaceful uses. Perhaps it will become a source of power for certain purposes, thus carrying further the concentration at present represented by power stations. Perhaps it will be used as the Soviet Government says it intends to use it—to alter physical geography by abolishing mountains and turning deserts into lakes. But as far as can be judged at present, atomic energy is not likely to be as important in peace as in war.

War has been, throughout history, the chief source of social cohesion; and since science began, it has been the strongest incentive to technical progress. Large groups have a better chance of victory than small ones, and therefore the usual result of war is to make States larger. In any given state of technique there is a limit to size. The Roman Empire was stopped by German forests and African deserts; the British conquests in India were halted by the Himalayas; Napoleon was defeated by the Russian winter. And before the telegraph large empires tended to break up because they could not be effectively controlled from a center.

Communications have been hitherto the chief factor limiting the size of empires. In antiquity the Persians and the Romans depended upon roads, but since nothing traveled faster than a horse, empires became unmanageable when the distance from the capital to the frontier was very great. This difficulty was diminished by railways and the telegraph, and is on the point of disappearing with the improvement of the long-range bomber. There would now be no technical difficulty about a single world-wide Empire. Since war is likely to become more destructive of human life than it has been in recent centuries, unification under a single government is probably necessary unless we are to acquiesce in either a return to barbarism or the extinction of the human race.

There is, it must be confessed, a psychological difficulty about a single world government. The chief source of social cohesion in the past, I repeat, has been war: the passions that inspire a feeling of unity are hate and fear. These depend upon the existence of an enemy, actual or potential. It seems to follow that a world government could only be kept in being by force, not by the spontaneous loyalty that now inspires a nation at war. I will return to this problem at a later stage.

So far, I have been considering only techniques derived from physics and chemistry. These have, up to the present, been the most important, but biology, physiology, and psychology are likely in the long run to affect human life quite as much as physics and chemistry.

Take first the question of food and population. At present the population of the globe is increasing at the rate of about 20 millions a year. Most of this increase is in Russia and Southeast Asia. The population of Western Europe and the United States is nearly stationary. Meanwhile, the food supply of the world as a whole threatens to diminish, as a result of unwise methods of cultivation and destruction of forests. This is an explosive situation. Left to itself, it must lead to a food shortage and thence to a world war. Technique, however, makes other issues possible.

Vital statistics in the West are dominated by medicine and birth control: the one diminishes the deaths, the other the births. The result is that the average age in the West increases: there is a smaller percentage of young people and a larger percentage of old people. Some people consider that this must have unfortunate results, but speaking as an old person, I am not sure.

The danger of a world shortage of food may be averted for a time by improvements in the technique of agriculture. But, if population continues to increase at the present rate, such improvements cannot long suffice. There will then be two groups, one poor with an increasing population, the other rich with a stationary population. Such a situation can hardly fail to lead to world war. If there is not to be an endless succession of wars, population will have to become stationary throughout the world, and this will probably have to be done, in many countries, as a result of governmental measures. This will require an extension of scientific technique into very intimate matters. There are, however, two other possibilities. War may become so destructive that, at any rate for a time, there is no danger of overpopulation; or the scientific nations may be defeated and anarchy may destroy scientific technique.

Biology is likely to affect human life through the study of heredity. Without science, men have changed domestic animals and food plants enormously in advantageous ways. It may be assumed that they will change them much more, and much more quickly, by bringing the science of genetics to bear. Perhaps, even, it may become possible artificially to induce desirable mutations in genes. (Hitherto the only mutations that can be artificially caused are neutral or harmful.) In any case, it is pretty certain that scientific technique will very soon effect great improvements in the animals and plants that are useful to man.

When such methods of modifying the congenital character of animals and plants have been pursued long enough to make their success obvious, it is probable that there will be a powerful movement for applying scientific methods to human propagation. There would at first be strong religious and emotional obstacles to the adoption of such a policy. But suppose (say) Russia were able to overcome these obstacles and to breed a race stronger, more intelligent, and more resistant to disease than any race of men that has hitherto existed, and suppose the other nations perceived that unless they followed suit they would be defeated in war, then either the other nations would voluntarily forgo their prejudices, or, after defeat, they would be compelled to forgo them. Any scientific technique, however beastly, is bound to spread if it is useful in war—until such time as men decide that they have had enough of war and will henceforth live in peace. As that day does not seem to be at hand, scientific breeding of human beings must be expected to come about. I shall return to this subject in a later chapter.

Physiology and psychology afford fields for scientific technique which still await development. Two great men, Pavlov and Freud, have laid the foundation. I do not accept the view that they are in any essential conflict, but what structure will be built on their foundations is still in doubt.

I think the subject which will be of most importance politically is mass psychology. Mass psychology is, scientifically speaking, not a very advanced study, and so far its professors have not been in universities: they have been advertisers, politicians, and, above all, dictators. This study is immensely useful to practical men, whether they wish to become rich or to acquire the government. It is, of course, as a science, founded upon individual psychology, but hitherto it has employed rule-of-thumb methods which were based upon a kind of intuitive common sense. Its importance has been enormously increased by the growth of modern methods of propaganda. Of these the most influential is what is called "education." Religion plays a part, though a diminishing one; the press, the cinema, and the radio play an increasing part.

What is essential in mass psychology is the art of persuasion. If you compare a speech of Hitler's with a speech of (say) Edmund Burke, you will see what strides have been made in the art since the eighteenth century. What went wrong formerly was that people had read in books that man is a rational animal, and framed their arguments on this hypothesis. We now know that limelight and a brass band do more to persuade than can be done by the most elegant train of syllogisms. It may be hoped that in time anybody will be able to persuade anybody of anything if he can catch the patient young and is provided by the State with money and equipment.

This subject will make great strides when it is taken up by scientists under a scientific dictatorship. Anaxagoras maintained that snow is black, but no one believed him. The social psychologists of the future will have a number of classes of school children on whom they will try different methods of producing an unshakable conviction that snow is black. Various results will soon be arrived at. First, that the influence of home is obstructive. Second, that not much can be done unless indoctrination begins before the age of ten. Third, that verses set to music and repeatedly intoned are very effective. Fourth, that the opinion that snow is white must be held to show a morbid taste for eccentricity. But I anticipate. It is for future scientists to make these maxims precise and discover exactly how much it costs per head to make children believe that snow is black, and how much less it would cost to make them believe it is dark gray.

Although this science will be diligently studied, it will be rigidly confined to the governing class. The populace will not be allowed to know how its convictions were generated. When the technique has been perfected, every government that has been in charge of education for a generation will be able to control its subjects securely without the need of armies or policemen. As yet there is only one country which has succeeded in creating this politician's paradise.

The social effects of scientific technique have already been many and important, and are likely to be even more note-worthy in the future. Some of these effects depend upon the political and economic character of the country concerned; others are inevitable, whatever this character may be. I propose in this chapter to consider only the inevitable effects.

The most obvious and inescapable effect of scientific technique is that it makes society more organic, in the sense of increasing the interdependence of its various parts. In the sphere of production, this has two forms. There is first the very intimate interconnection of individuals engaged in a common enterprise, e.g. in a single factory; and secondly there is the relation, less intimate but still essential, between one enterprise and another. Each of these becomes more important with every advance in scientific technique.

A peasant in an unindustrialized country may produce almost all his own food by means of very inexpensive tools. These tools, some of his clothes, and a few things such as salt are all that he needs to buy. His relations with the outer world are thus reduced to a minimum. So long as he produces, with the help of his wife and children, a little more food than the family requires, he can enjoy almost complete independence, though at the cost of hardship and poverty. But in a time of famine he goes hungry, and probably most of his children die. His liberty is so dearly bought that few civilized men would change places with him. This was the lot of most of the population of civilized countries till the rise of industrialism.

Although the peasant's lot is in any case a hard one, it is apt to be rendered harder by one or both of two enemies: the moneylender and the landowner. In any history of any period, you will find roughly the following gloomy picture: "At this time the old hardy yeoman stock had fallen upon evil days. Under threat of starvation from bad harvests, many of them had borrowed from urban landowners, who had none of their traditions, their ancient piety, or their patient courage. Those who had taken this fatal step became, almost inevitably, the slaves or serfs of members of the new commercial class. And so the sturdy farmers, who had been the backbone of the nation, were submerged by supple men who had the skill to amass new wealth by dubious methods." You will find substantially this account in the history of Attica before Solon, of Latium after the Punic Wars, of England in the early nineteenth century, of Southern California as depicted in Norris' *Octopus*, of India under the British Raj, and of the reasons which have led Chinese peasants to support communism. The process, however regrettable, is an unavoidable stage in the integration of agriculture into a larger economy.

By way of contrast with the primitive peasant, consider the agrarian interests in modern California or Canada or Australia or the Argentine. Everything is produced for export, and the prosperity to be brought by exporting depends upon such distant matters as war in Europe or Marshall Aid or the devaluation of the pound. Everything turns on politics, on whether the Farm Bloc is strong in Washington, whether there is reason to fear that Argentina may make friends with Russia, and so on. There may still be nominally independent farmers, but in fact they are in the power of the vast financial interests that are concerned in manipulating political issues. This interdependence is in no degree lessened—perhaps it is even increased—if the countries concerned are socialist, as, for example, if the Soviet Government and the British Government make a deal to exchange food for machinery. All this is the effect of scientific technique in agriculture. Malthus, at the beginning of the nineteenth century, wrote: "In the wildness of speculation it has been suggested (of course more in jest than in earnest) that Europe should grow its corn in America, and devote itself solely to manufactures and commerce." It turned out that the speculation was by no means "wild."

So much for agriculture. In industry, the integration brought about by scientific technique is much greater and more intimate.

One of the most obvious results of industrialism is that a much larger percentage of the population live in towns than was formerly the case. The town dweller is a more social being than the agriculturist, and is much more influenced by discussion. In general, he works in a crowd, and his amusements are apt to take him into still larger crowds. The course of nature, the alternations of day and night, summer and winter, wet or shine, make little difference to him; he has no occasion to fear that he will be ruined by frost or drought or sudden rain. What matters to him is his human environment, and his place in various organizations especially.

Take a man who works in a factory, and consider how many organizations affect his life. There is first of all the factory itself, and any larger organization of which it may be a part. Then there is the man's trade union and his political party. He probably gets house room from a building society or public authority. His children go to school. If he reads a newspaper or goes to a cinema or looks at a football match, these things are provided by powerful organizations. Indirectly, through his employers, he is dependent upon those from whom they buy their raw material and those to whom they sell their finished product. Above all, there is the State, which taxes him and may at any moment order him to go and get killed in war, in return for which it protects him against murder and theft so long as there is peace, and allows him to buy a fixed modicum of food.

The capitalist in modern England, as he is never weary of telling us, is equally hemmed in. Half, or more than half, of his profits go to a government that he detests. His investing is severely controlled. He needs permits for everything, and has to show cause why he should get them. The government has views as to where he should sell. His raw material may be very difficult to get, particularly if it comes from a dollar area. In all dealings with his employees he has to be careful to avoid stirring up a strike. He is haunted by fear of a slump, and wonders whether he will be able to keep up the premiums on his life insurance. He wakes in the night in a cold sweat, having dreamed that war has broken out and his factory and his house and his wife and his children have all been wiped out. But, although his liberty is destroyed by such a multiplicity of organizations, he is busy trying to make more of them: new armed units, Western Union, Atlantic Pact, lobbies, and fighting unions of manufacturers. In nostalgic moments he may talk about *laisser faire*, but in fact he sees no hope of safety except in new organizations to fight existing ones that he dislikes, for he knows that as an isolated unit he would be powerless, and as an isolated State his country would be powerless.

The increase of organization has brought into existence new positions of power. Every body has to have executive officials, in whom, at any moment, its power is concentrated. It is true that officials are usually subject to control, but the control may be slow and distant. From the young lady who sells stamps in a post office all the way up to the Prime Minister, every official is invested, for the time being, with some part of the power of the State. You can complain of the young lady if her manners are bad, and you can vote against the Prime Minister at the next election if you disapprove of his policy. But both the young lady and the Prime Minister can have a very considerable run for their money before (if ever) your discontent has any effect. This increase in the power of officials is a constant source of irritation to everybody else. In most countries they are much less polite than in England; the police, especially in America for instance, seem to think you must be a rare exception if you are not a criminal. This tyranny of officials is one of the worst results of increasing organization, and one against which it is of the utmost importance to find safeguards if a scientific society is not to be intolerable to all but an insolent aristocracy of Jacks-in-office. But for the present I am concerned with description, not with schemes of reform.

The power of officials is, usually, distinct from that of people who are theoretically in ultimate control. In large corporations, although the directors are nominally elected by the shareholders, they usually manage, by various devices, to be in fact self-perpetuating, and to acquire new directors, when necessary, by co-option more or less disguised as election. In British politics, it is a commonplace that most Ministers find it impossible to cope with their civil servants, who in effect dictate policy except on party questions that have been prominently before the public. In many countries the armed forces are apt to get out of hand and defy the civil authorities. Of the police I have already spoken, but concerning them there is more to be said. In countries where the communists enter coalition governments, they always endeavor to make sure of control of the police. When once this is secured, they can manufacture plots, make arrests, and extort confessions freely. By this means they pass from being participants in a coalition to being the whole government. The problem of causing the police to obey the law is a very difficult one; it is, for example, very far from being solved in America, where confessions are apt to be extorted by "third degree" from people who may well be innocent.[1]

The increased power of officials is an inevitable result of the greater degree of organization that scientific technique brings about. It has the drawback that it is apt to be irresponsible, behind-the-scenes, power, like that of emperors' eunuchs and kings' mistresses in former times. To discover ways of controlling it is one of the most important political problems of our time. Liberals protested, successfully, against the power of kings and aristocrats; socialists protested against the power of capitalists. But unless the power of officials can be kept within bounds, socialism will mean little more than the substitution of one set of masters for another: all the former power of the capitalist will be inherited by the official. In 1942, when I lived in the country in America, I had a part-time gardener, who spent the bulk of his working day making munitions. He told me with triumph that his union had secured the "closed shop." A little while later he told me, without triumph, that the union dues had been raised and that the extra money went wholly to increase the salary of the secretary of the union. Owing to what was practically a war situation between labor and capital, any agitation against the secretary could be represented as treachery. This little story illustrates the helplessness of the public against its own officials, even where there is nominally complete democracy.

One of the drawbacks to the power of officials is that they are apt to be quite remote from the things they control.

[1] See *Our Lawless Police*, by Ernest Jerome Hopkins, N.Y., Viking Press.

What do the men in the Education Office know about education? Only what they dimly remember of their public school and university some twenty or thirty years ago. What does the Ministry of Agriculture know about mangel-wurzels? Only how they are spelled. What does the Foreign Office know about modern China? After I had returned from China in 1921, I had some dealings with the permanent officials who determined British Far Eastern policy, and found their ignorance unsurpassed except by their conceit. America has invented the phrase "yes-men" for those who flatter great executives. In England we are more troubled by "no-men," who make it their business to employ clever ignorance in opposing and sabotaging every scheme suggested by those who have knowledge and imagination and enterprise. I am afraid our "no-men" are a thousand times more harmful than the American "yes-men." If we are to recover prosperity, we shall have to find ways of emancipating energy and enterprise from the frustrating control of constitutionally timid ignoramuses.

Owing to increase of organization, the question of the limits of individual liberty needs completely different treatment from that of nineteenth-century writers such as Mill. The acts of a single man are as a rule unimportant, but the acts of groups are more important than they used to be. Take, for example, refusal to work. If one man, on his own initiative, chooses to be idle, that may be regarded as his own affair; he loses his wages, and there is an end of the matter. But if there is a strike in a vital industry, the whole community suffers. I am not arguing that the right to strike should be abolished; I am only arguing that, if it is to be preserved, it must be for reasons concerned with this particular matter, and not on general grounds of personal liberty. In a highly organized country there are many activities which are important to everybody, and without which there would be widespread hardship. Matters should be so arranged that large groups seldom think it to their interest to strike. This can be done by arbitration and conciliation, or, as under the dictatorship of the proletariat, by starvation and police action. But in one way or another it must be done if an industrial society is to prosper.

War is a more extreme case than strikes, but raises very similar questions of principle. When two men fight a duel, the matter is trivial, but when 200 million people fight 200 million other people the matter is serious. And with every increase of organization war becomes more serious. Until the present century, the great majority of the population, even in nations engaged in such contests as the Napoleonic Wars, were still occupied with peaceful pursuits, and as a rule little disturbed in their ordinary habits of life. Now, almost everybody, women as well as men, are set to some kind of war work. The resulting dislocation makes the peace, when it comes, almost worse than the war. Since the end of the late war, throughout Central Europe, enormous numbers, men, women, and children, have died in circumstances of appalling suffering, and many millions of survivors have become homeless wanderers, uprooted, without work, without hope, a burden equally to themselves and to those who feed them. This sort of thing is to be expected when defeat introduces chaos into highly organized communities.

The right to make war, like the right to strike, but in a far higher degree, is very dangerous in a world governed by scientific technique. Neither can be simply abolished, since that would open the road to tyranny. But in each case it must be recognized that groups cannot, in the name of freedom, justly claim the right to inflict great injuries upon others. As regards war, the principle of unrestricted national sovereignty, cherished by liberals in the nineteenth century and by the Kremlin in the present day, must be abandoned. Means must be found of subjecting the relations of nations to the rule of law, so that a single nation will no longer be, as at present, the judge in its own cause. If this is not done, the world will quickly return to barbarism. If that case, scientific technique will disappear along with science, and men will be able to go on being quarrelsome because their quarrels will no longer do much harm. It is, however, just possible that mankind may prefer to survive and prosper rather than to perish in misery, and, if so, national liberty will have to be effectively restrained.

As we have seen, the question of freedom needs a completely fresh examination. There are forms of freedom that are desirable, and that are gravely threatened; there are other forms of freedom that are undesirable, but that are very difficult to curb. There are two dangers, both rapidly increasing. Within any given organization, the power of officials, or of what may be called the "government," tends to become excessive, and to subject individuals to various forms of tyranny. On the other hand, conflicts between different organizations become more and more harmful as organizations acquire more power over their members. Tyranny within and conflict without are each other's counterpart. Both spring from the same source: the lust for power. A State which is internally despotic will be externally warlike, in both respects because the men who govern the State desire the greatest attainable extent and intensity of control over the lives of other men. The resultant twofold problem, of preserving liberty internally and diminishing it externally, is one that the world must solve, and solve soon, if scientific societies are to survive.

Let us consider for a moment the social psychology involved in this situation.

Organizations are of two kinds, those which aim at getting something done, and those which aim at preventing something from being done. The Post Office is an example of the first kind; a fire brigade is an example of the second kind. Neither of these arouses much controversy, because no one objects to letters' being carried, and incendiaries dare not avow a desire to see buildings burnt down. But when what is to be prevented is something done by human beings, not by Nature, the matter is otherwise. The armed forces of one's own nation exist—so each nation asserts—to *prevent* aggression by other nations. But the armed forces of other nations exist—or so many people believe—to *promote* aggression. If you say anything against the armed forces of your own country, you are a traitor, wishing to see your fatherland ground under the heel of a brutal conqueror. If, on the other hand, you defend a potential enemy State for thinking armed forces necessary to its safety, you malign your own country, whose unalterable devotion to peace only perverse malice could lead you to question. I heard all this said about Germany by a thoroughly virtuous German lady in 1936, in the course of a panegyric on Hitler.

The same sort of thing applies, though with slightly less force, to other combatant organizations. My Pennsylvania gardener would not publicly criticize his trade union secretary for fear of weakening the union in contest with capitalists. It is difficult for a man of ardent political convictions to admit either the shortcomings of politicians of his own Party or the merits of those of the opposite Party.

And so it comes about that, whenever an organization has a combatant purpose, its members are reluctant to criticize their officials, and tend to acquiesce in usurpations and arbitrary exercises of power which, but for the war mentality, they would bitterly resent. It is the war mentality that gives officials and governments their opportunity. It is therefore only natural that officials and governments are prone to foster war mentality.

The only escape is to have the greatest possible number of disputes settled by legal process, and not by a trial of strength. Thus here again the preservation of internal liberty and external control go hand in hand, and both equally depend upon what is *prima facie* a restraint upon liberty, namely an extension of the domain of law and of the public force necessary for its enforcement.

In what I have been saying so far in this chapter I feel that I have not sufficiently emphasized the gains that we derive from scientific technique. It is obvious that the average inhabitant of the United States at the present day is very much richer than the average inhabitant of England in the eighteenth century, and this advance is almost entirely due to scientific technique. The gain in the case of England is not so great, but that is because we have spent so much on killing Germans. But even in England there are enormous material advances. In spite of shortages, almost everybody has as much to eat as is necessary for health and efficiency. Most people have warmth in winter and adequate light after sunset. The streets, except in time of war, are not pitch dark at night. All children go to school. Everyone can get medical attendance. Life and property are much more secure (in peacetime) than they were in the eighteenth century. A much smaller percentage of the population lives in slums.

Travel is vastly easier, and many more amusements are available than in former times. The improvement in health would in itself be sufficient to make this age preferable to those earlier times for which some people feel nostalgic. On the whole, I think, this age is an improvement on all its predecessors except for the rich and privileged.

Our advantages are due entirely, or almost entirely, to the fact that a given amount of labor is more productive than it was in pre-scientific days. I used to live on a hilltop surrounded by trees, where I could pick up firewood with the greatest ease. But to secure a given amount of fuel in this way cost more human labor than to have it brought across half England in the form of coal, because the coal was mined and brought scientifically, whereas I could employ only primitive methods in gathering sticks. In old days, one man produced not much more than one man's necessaries; a tiny aristocracy lived in luxury, a small middle class lived in moderate comfort, but the great majority of the population had very little more than was required in order to keep alive. It is true that we do not always spend our surplus of labor wisely. We are able to set aside a much larger proportion for war than our ancestors could. But almost all the large-scale disadvantages of our time arise from failure to extend the domain of law to the settlement of disputes which, when left to the arbitrament of force, have become, through our very efficiency, more harmful than in previous centuries. This survival of formerly endurable anarchy must be dealt with if our civilization is to survive. Where liberty is harmful, it is to law that we must look.

CHAPTER III

Scientific Technique in
an Oligarchy

I MEAN by "oligarchy" any system in which ultimate power is confined to a section of the community: the rich to the exclusion of the poor, Protestants to the exclusion of Catholics, aristocrats to the exclusion of plebeians, white men to the exclusion of colored men, males to the exclusion of females, or members of one political party to the exclusion of the rest. A system may be more oligarchic or less so, according to the percentage of the population that is excluded; absolute monarchy is the extreme of oligarchy.

Apart from masculine domination, which was universal until the present century, oligarchies in the past were usually based upon birth or wealth or race. A new kind of oligarchy was introduced by the Puritans during the English Civil War. They called it the "Rule of the Saints." It consisted essentially of confining the possession of arms to the adherents of one political creed, who were thus enabled to control the government in spite of being a minority without any traditional claim to power. This system, although in England it ended with the Restoration, was revived in Russia in 1918, in Italy in 1922, and in Germany in 1933. It is now the only vital form of oligarchy, and it is therefore the form that I shall specially consider.

We have seen that scientific technique increases the importance of organizations, and therefore the extent to which authority impinges upon the life of the individual. It follows that a scientific oligarchy has more power than any oligarchy could have in pre-scientific times. There is a tendency, which is inevitable unless consciously combated, for organizations to coalesce, and so to increase in size, until, ultimately, almost all become merged in the State. A scientific oligarchy, accordingly, is bound to become what is called "totalitarian," that is to say, all important forms of power will become a monopoly of the State. This monolithic system has sufficient merits to be attractive to many people, but to my mind its demerits are far greater than its merits. For some reason which I have failed to understand, many people like the system when it is Russian but disliked the very same system when it was German. I am compelled to think that this is due to the power of labels; these people like whatever is labeled "Left" without examining whether the label has any justification.

Oligarchies, throughout past history, have always thought more of their own advantage than of that of the rest of the community. It would be foolish to be morally indignant with them on this account; human nature, in the main and in the mass, is egoistic, and in most circumstances a fair dose of egoism is necessary for survival. It was revolt against the selfishness of past political oligarchies that produced the Liberal movement in favor of democracy, and it was revolt against economic oligarchies that produced socialism. But although everybody who was in any degree progressive recognized the evils of oligarchy throughout the past history of mankind, many progressives were taken in by an argument for a new kind of oligarchy. "We, the progressives"—so runs the argument—"are the wise and good; we know what reforms the world needs; if we have power, we shall create a paradise." And so, narcissistically hypnotized by contemplation of their own wisdom and goodness, they proceeded to create a new tyranny, more drastic than any previously known. It is the effect of science in such a system that I wish to consider in this chapter.

In the first place, since the new oligarchs are the adherents of a certain creed, and base their claim to exclusive power upon the rightness of this creed, their system depends essentially upon dogma: whoever questions the governmental dogma questions the moral authority of the government, and is therefore a rebel. While the oligarchy is still new, there are sure to be other creeds, held with equal conviction, which would seize the government if they could. Such rival creeds must be suppressed by force, since the principle of majority rule has been abandoned. It follows that there cannot be freedom of the press, freedom of discussion, or freedom of book publication. There must be an organ of government whose duty it is to pronounce as to what is orthodox, and to punish heresy. The history of the Inquisition shows what such an organ of government must inevitably become. In the normal pursuit of power, it will seek out more and more subtle heresies. The Church, as soon as it acquired political power, developed incredible refinements of dogma, and persecuted what to us appear microscopic deviations from the official creed. Exactly the same sort of thing happens in the modern States that confine political power to supporters of a certain doctrine.

The completeness of the resulting control over opinion

depends in various ways upon scientific technique. Where all children go to school, and all schools are controlled by the government, the authorities can close the minds of the young to everything contrary to official orthodoxy. Printing is impossible without paper, and all paper belongs to the State. Broadcasting and the cinema are equally public monopolies. The only remaining possibility of unauthorized propaganda is by secret whispers from one individual to another. But this, in turn, is rendered appallingly dangerous by improvements in the art of spying. Children at school are taught that it is their duty to denounce their parents if they allow themselves subversive utterances in the bosom of the family. No one can be sure that a man who seems to be his dearest friend will not denounce him to the police; the man may himself have been in some trouble, and may know that if he is not efficient as a spy his wife and children will suffer. All this is not imaginary; it is daily and hourly reality. Nor, given oligarchy, is there the slightest reason to expect anything else.

People still shudder at the enormities of men like Caligula and Nero, but their misdeeds fade into insignificance beside those of modern tyrants. Except among the upper classes in Rome, daily life was much as usual even under the worst emperors. Caligula wished his enemies had but a single head; how he would have envied Hitler the scientific lethal chambers of Auschwitz! Nero did his best to establish a spy system which would smell out traitors, but a conspiracy defeated him in the end. If he had been defended by the N.K.V.D. he might have died in his bed at a ripe old age. These are a few of the blessings that science has bestowed on tyrants.

Consider next the economic system appropriate to an oligarchy. We in England had such a system in the early nineteenth century; how abominable it was, you can read in the Hammonds' books. It came to an end, chiefly owing to the quarrel between landowners and industrialists. Landowners befriended the wage-earners in towns, and industrialists befriended those in the country. Between the two, factory Acts were passed and the Corn Laws were repealed. In the end we adopted democracy, which made a modicum of economic justice unavoidable.

In Russia the development has been different. The government fell into the hands of the self-professed champions of the proletariat, who, as a result of civil war, were able to establish a military dictatorship. Gradually irresponsible power produced its usual effect. Those who commanded the army and the police saw no occasion for economic justice; soldiers were sent to take grain by force from starving peasants, who died by millions as a result. Wage-earners, deprived of the right to strike, and without the possibility of electing representatives to plead their cause, were kept down to bare subsistence level. The percentage difference between the pay of army officers and that of privates is vastly greater in Russia than in any Western country. Men who hold important positions in business live in luxury; the ordinary employee suffers as much as in England one hundred and fifty years ago. But even he is still among the more fortunate.

Underneath the system of so-called "free" labor there is another: the system of forced labor and concentration camps. The life of the victims of this system is unspeakable. The hours are unbearably long, the food only just enough to keep the laborers alive for a year or so, the clothing in an arctic winter so scanty that it would barely suffice in an English summer. Men and women are seized in their homes in the middle of the night; there is no trial, and often no charge is formulated; they disappear, and inquiries by their families remain unanswered; after a year or two in Northeast Siberia or on the shores of the White Sea, they die of cold, overwork, and undernourishment. But that causes no concern to the authorities; there are plenty more to come.

This terrible system is rapidly growing. The number of people condemned to forced labor is a matter of conjecture; some say that 16 per cent of the adult males in the U.S.S.R. are involved, and all competent authorities (except the Soviet Government and its friends) are agreed that it is at least 8 per cent. The proportion of women and children, though large, is much less than that of adult males.

Inevitably, forced labor, because it is economical, is favorably viewed by the authorities, and tends, by its competition, to depress the condition of "free" laborers. In the nature of things, unless the system is swept away, it must grow until no one is outside it except the army, the police, and government officials.

From the standpoint of the national economy, the system has great advantages. It has made possible the construction of the Baltic–White Sea canal and the sale of timber in exchange for machinery. It has increased the surplus of labor available for war production. By the terror that it inspires it has diminished disaffection. But these are small matters compared to what—we are told—is to be accomplished in the near future. Atomic energy is to be employed (so at least it is said) to divert the waters of the River Yenisei, which now flow fruitlessly into the Arctic, so as to cause them to bestow fertility on a vast desert region in Central Asia.

But if, when this work is completed, Russia is still subject to a small despotic aristocracy, there is no reason to expect that the masses will be allowed to benefit. It will be found that radioactive spray can be used to melt the Polar ice, or that a range of mountains in northern Siberia would divert the cold north winds, and could be constructed at a cost in human misery which would not be thought excessive. And whenever other ways of disposing of the surplus fail, there is always war. So long as the rulers are comfortable, what reason have they to improve the lot of their serfs?

I think the evils that have grown up in Soviet Russia will exist, in a greater or less degree, wherever there is a scientific government which is securely established and is not dependent upon popular support. It is possible nowadays for a government to be very much more oppressive than any government could be before there was scientific technique. Propaganda makes persuasion easier for the government; public ownership of halls and paper makes counterpropaganda more difficult; and the effectiveness of modern armaments makes popular risings impossible. No revolution can succeed in a modern country unless it has the support of at least a considerable section of the armed forces. But the armed forces can be kept loyal by being given a higher standard of life than that of the average worker, and this is made easier by every step in the degradation of ordinary labor. Thus the very evils of the system help to give it stability. Apart from external pressure, there is no reason why such a regime should not last for a very long time.

Scientific societies are as yet in their infancy. It may be worth while to spend a few moments in speculating as to possible future developments of those that are oligarchies.

It is to be expected that advances in physiology and psychology will give governments much more control over individual mentality than they now have even in totalitarian countries. Fichte laid it down that education should aim at destroying free will, so that, after pupils have left school, they shall be incapable, throughout the rest of their lives, of thinking or acting otherwise than as their schoolmasters would have wished. But in his day this was an unattainable ideal: what he regarded as the best system in existence produced Karl Marx. In future such failures are not likely to occur where there is dictatorship. Diet, injections, and injunctions will combine, from a very early age, to produce the sort of character and the sort of beliefs that the authorities consider desirable, and any serious criticism of the powers that be will become psychologically impossible. Even if all are miserable, all will believe themselves happy, because the government will tell them that they are so.

A totalitarian government with a scientific bent might do things that to us would seem horrifying. The Nazis were more scientific than the present rulers of Russia, and were more inclined towards the sort of atrocities than I have in mind. They were said—I do not know with what truth—to use prisoners in concentration camps as material for all kinds of experiments, some involving death after much pain. If they had survived, they would probably have soon taken to scientific breeding. Any nation which adopts this practice will, within a generation, secure great military advantages. The system, one may surmise, will be something like this: except possibly in the governing aristocracy, all but 5 per cent of males and 30 per cent of females will be sterilized. The 30 per cent of females will be expected to spend the years from eighteen to forty in reproduction, in order to secure adequate cannon fodder. As a rule, artificial insemination will be preferred to the natural method. The unsterilized, if they desire the pleasures of love, will usually have to seek them with sterilized partners.

Sires will be chosen for various qualities, some for muscle, others for brains. All will have to be healthy, and unless they are to be the fathers of oligarchs they will have to be of a submissive and docile disposition. Children will, as in Plato's *Republic*, be taken from their mothers and reared by professional nurses. Gradually, by selective breeding, the congenital differences between rulers and ruled will increase until they become almost different species. A revolt of the plebs would become as unthinkable as an organized insurrection of sheep against the practice of eating mutton. (The Aztecs kept a domesticated alien tribe for purposes of cannibalism. Their regime was totalitarian.)

To those accustomed to this system, the family as we know it would seem as queer as the tribal and totem organization of Australian aborigines seems to us. Freud would have to be rewritten, and I incline to think that Adler would be found more relevant. The laboring class would have such long hours of work and so little to eat that their desires would hardly extend beyond sleep and food. The upper class, being deprived of the softer pleasures both by the abolition of the family and by the supreme duty of devotion to the State, would acquire the mentality of ascetics: they would care only for power, and in pursuit of it would not shrink from cruelty. By the practice of cruelty men would become hardened, so that worse and worse tortures would be required to give the spectators a thrill.

Such possibilities, on any large scale, may seem a fantastic nightmare. But I firmly believe that, if the Nazis had won the last war, and if in the end they had acquired world supremacy they would, before long, have established just such a system as I have been suggesting. They would have used Russians and Poles as robots, and when their empire was secure they would have used also Negroes and Chinese. Western nations would have been converted into becoming collaborationists, by the methods practiced in France from 1940 to 1944. Thirty years of these methods would have left the West with little inclination to rebel.

To prevent these scientific horrors, democracy is necessary but not sufficient. There must be also that kind of respect for the individual that inspired the doctrine of the Rights of Man. As an absolute theory the doctrine cannot be accepted. As Bentham said: "Rights of man, nonsense; imprescriptible rights of man, nonsense on stilts." We must admit that there are gains to the community so great that for their sake it becomes right to inflict an injustice on an individual. This may happen, to take an obvious example, if a victorious enemy demands hostages as the price of not destroying a city. The city authorities (not of course the enemy) cannot be blamed, in such circumstances, if they deliver the required number of hostages. In general, the "Rights of Man" must be subject to the supreme consideration of the general welfare. But having admitted this we must go on to assert, and to assert emphatically, that there are injuries which it is hardly ever in the general interest to inflict on innocent individuals. The doctrine is important because the holders of power, especially in an oligarchy, will be much too prone, on each occasion, to think that this is one of those cases in which the doctrine should be ignored.

Totalitariansim has a theory as well as a practice. As a practice, it means that a certain group, having by one means or another seized the apparatus of power, especially armaments and police, proceed to exploit their advantageous position to the utmost, by regulating everything in the way that gives them the maximum of control over others. But as a theory it is something different: it is the doctrine that the State, or the nation, or the community is capable of a good different from that of individuals, and not consisting of anything that individuals think or feel. This doctrine was especially advocated by Hegel, who glorified the State, and thought that a community should be as organic as possible. In an organic community, he thought, excellence would reside in the whole. An individual is an organism, and we do not think that his separate parts have separate goods: if he has a pain in his great toe it is he that suffers, not specially the great toe. So, in an organic society, good and evil will belong to the whole rather than the parts. This is the theoretical form of totalitarianism.

The difficulty about this theory is that it extends illegitimately the analogy between a social organism and a single person as an organism. The government, as opposed to its individual members, is not sentient; it does not rejoice at a victory or suffer at a defeat. When the body politic is injured, whatever pain is to be felt must be felt by its members, not by it as a whole. With the body of a single person it is otherwise: all pains are felt at the center. If the different parts of the body had pains that the central ego did not feel, they might have their separate interests, and need a Parliament to decide whether the toes should give way to the fingers or the fingers to the toes. As this is not the case, a single person is an ethical unit. Neither parts of a person nor organizations of many persons can occupy the same position of ethical importance. The good of a multitude is a sum of the goods of the individuals composing it, not a new and separate good. In concrete fact, when it is pretended that the State has a good different from that of the citizens, what is really meant is that the good of the government or of the ruling class is more important than that of other people. Such a view can have no basis except in arbitrary power.

More important than these metaphysical speculations is the question whether a scientific dictatorship, such as we have been considering, can be stable, or is more likely to be stable than a democracy.

Apart from the danger of war, I see no reason why such a regime should be unstable. After all, most civilized and semi-civilized countries known to history have had a large class of slaves or serfs completely subordinate to their owners. There is nothing in human nature that makes the persistence of such a system impossible. And the whole development of scientific technique has made it easier than it used to be to maintain a despotic rule of a minority. When the government controls the distribution of food, its power is absolute so long as it can count on the police and the armed forces. And their loyalty can be secured by giving them some of the privileges of the governing class. I do not see how any internal movement of revolt can ever bring freedom to the oppressed in a modern scientific dictatorship.

But when it comes to external war the matter is different. Given two countries with equal natural resources, one a dictatorship and the other allowing individual liberty, the one allowing liberty is almost certain to become superior to the other in war technique in no very long time. As we have seen in Germany and Russia, freedom in scientific research is incompatible with dictatorship. Germany might well have won the war if Hitler could have endured Jewish physicists. Russia will have less grain than if Stalin had not insisted upon the adoption of Lysenko's theories. It is highly probable that there will soon be, in Russia, a similar governmental incursion into the domain of nuclear physics. I do not doubt that, if there is no war during the next fifteen years, Russian scientific war technique will, at the end of that time, be very markedly inferior to that of the West, and that the inferiority will be directly traceable to dictatorship. I think, therefore, that, so long as powerful democracies exist, democracy will in the long run be victorious. And on this basis I allow myself a moderate optimism as to the future. Scientific dictatorships will perish through not being sufficiently scientific.

We may perhaps go further: the causes which will make dictatorships lag behind in science will also generate other weaknesses. All new ideas will come to be viewed as heresy, so that there will be a lack of adaptability to new circumstances. The governing class will tend to become lazy as soon as it feels secure. If, on the other hand, initiative is encouraged in the people near the top, there will be constant danger of palace revolutions. One of the troubles in the late Roman Empire was that a successful general could, with luck, make himself Emperor, so that the reigning Emperor always had a motive for putting successful generals to death. This sort of trouble can easily arise in a dictatorship, as events have already proved.

For these various reasons, I do not believe that dictatorship is a lasting form of scientific society—unless (but this proviso is important) it can become world-wide.

CHAPTER IV

Democracy and Scientific Technique

THE word "democracy" has become ambiguous. East of the Elbe it means "military dictatorship of a minority enforced by arbitrary police power." West of the Elbe its meaning is less definite, but broadly speaking it means "even distribution of ultimate political power among all adults except lunatics, criminals, and peers." This is not a precise definition, because of the word "ultimate." Suppose the British Constitution were to be changed in only one respect: that General Elections should occur once in thirty years instead of once in five. This would so much diminish the dependence of Parliament on public opinion that the resulting system could hardly be called a democracy. Many socialists would add economic to political power, as what demands even distribution in a democracy. But we may ignore these verbal questions. The essence of the matter is approach to equality of power, and it is obvious that democracy is a matter of degree.

When people think of democracy, they generally couple with it a considerable measure of liberty for individuals and groups. Religious persecution, for instance, would be excluded in imagination, although it is entirely compatible with democracy as defined a moment ago. I incline to think that "liberty," as the word was understood in the eighteenth and nineteenth centuries, is no longer quite the right concept; I should prefer to substitute "opportunity for initiative." And my reason for suggesting this change is the character of a scientific society.

It cannot be denied that democracy no longer inspires the same enthusiasm as it inspired in Rousseau and the men of the French Revolution. This is, of course, mainly because it has been achieved. Advocates of a reform always overstate their case, so that their converts expect the reform to bring the millennium. When it fails to do so there is disappointment, even if very solid advantages are secured. In France under Louis XVI many people thought that all evils proceeded from kings and priests, so they cut off the king's head and turned priests into hunted fugitives. But still they failed to enjoy celestial bliss. So they decided that although kings are bad there is no harm in emperors.

So it has been with democracy. Its sober advocates, notably Bentham and his school, maintained that it would do away with certain evils, and on the whole they proved right. But its enthusiasts, the followers of Rousseau especially, thought that it could achieve far more than there was good reason to expect. Its sober successes were forgotten, just because the evils which it had cured were no longer there to cause indignation. Consequently people listened to Carlyle's ridicule and Nietzsche's savage invective against it as the ethic of slaves. In many minds the cult of the hero replaced the cult of the common man. And the cult of the hero, in practice, is fascism.

The cult of the hero is anarchic and retrograde, and does

not easily fit in with the needs of a scientific society. But there is an opposite tendency, embodied in communism, which, though also antidemocratic, is in line with the technical developments of modern industry, and therefore much more worthy of consideration. This is the tendency to attach importance neither to heroes nor to common men, but to organizations. In this view the individual is nothing apart from the social bodies of which he is a member. Each such body—so it is said—represents some social force, and it is only as part of such a force that an individual is of importance.

We have thus three points of view, leading to three different political philosophies. You may view an individual, (a) as a common man, (b) as a hero, (c) as a cog in the machine. The first view leads you to old-fashioned democracy, the second to fascism, and the third to communism. I think that democracy, if it is to recover the power of inspiring vigorous action, needs to take account of what is valid in the other two way of regarding individuals.

Everybody exemplifies all three points of view in different situations. Even if you are the greatest of living poets, you are a common man where your ration book is concerned, or when you go to the polling booth to vote. However humdrum your daily life may be, there is a good chance that you will now and again have an opportunity for heroism: you may save someone from drowning, or (more likely) you may die nobly in battle. You are a cog in the machine if you work in an organized group, e.g. the army or the mining industry. What science has done is to increase the proportion of your life in which you are a cog, to the extent of endangering what is due to you as a hero or as a common man. The business of a modern advocate of democracy is to develop a political philosophy which avoids this danger.

In a good social system, every man will be at once a hero, a common man, and a cog, to the greatest possible extent, though if he is any one of these in an exceptional degree his other two roles may be diminished. *Qua* hero, a man should have the opportunity of initiative; *qua* common man, he should have security; *qua* cog, he should be useful. A nation cannot achieve great excellence by any one of these alone. In Poland before the partition, all were heroes (at least all nobles); the Middle West is the home of the common man; and in Russia everyone outside the Politburo is a cog. No one of these three is quite satisfactory.

The cog theory, though mechanically feasible, is humanly the most devastating of the three. A cog, we said, should be *useful*. Yes, but useful for what? You cannot say useful for promoting initiative, since the cog mentality is antithetic to the hero mentality. If you say useful for the happiness of the common man, you subordinate the machine to its effect in human feelings, which is to abandon the cog theory. You can only justify the cog theory by worship of the machine. You must make the machine an end in itself, not a means to what it produces. Human beings then become like slaves of the lamp in *The Arabian Nights*. It no longer matters what the machine produces, though on the whole bombs will be preferred to food because they require more elaborate mechanisms for their production. In time men will come to pray to the machine: "Almighty and most merciful Machine, we have erred and strayed from thy ways like lost screws; we have put in those nuts which we ought not to have put in, and we have left out those nuts which we ought to have put in, and there is no cogginess in us"—and so on.

This really won't do. The idolatry of the machine is an abomination. The Machine as an object of adoration is the modern form of Satan, and its worship is the modern diabolism.

Not that I wish, like the Erewhonians, to prohibit machines. The Egyptians worshiped bulls, which we think was a mistake, but we do not on that account prohibit bulls. It is only when the Machine takes the place of God that I object to it. Whatever else may be mechanical, values are not, and this is something which no political philosopher must forget.

But it is time to have done with these pleasant fancies and return to the subject of democracy.

The main point is this: Scientific technique, by making society more organic, increases the extent to which an individual is a cog; if this is not to be an evil, ways must be found of preventing him from being a *mere* cog. This means that initiative must be preserved in spite of organization. But most initiative will be what may be called in a large sense "political," that is to say, it will consist of advice as to what some organization should do. And if there is to be opportunity for this sort of initiative, organizations must, as far as possible, be governed democratically. Not only so, but the federal principle must be carried so far that every energetic person can hope to influence the government of *some* social group of which he is a member.

Democracy, at present, defeats its object by the vastness of the constituencies involved. Suppose you are an American, interested in a Presidential election. If you are a Senator or a Congressman, you can have a considerable influence, but the odds are about 100,000 to 1 that you are neither. If you are a ward politician you can do something. But if you are an ordinary citizen you can only vote. And I do not think there has ever been a Presidential election where one man's abstention would have altered the result. And so you feel as powerless as if you lived under a dictatorship. You are, of course, committing the classical fallacy of the heap, but most people's minds work that way.

In England it is not quite so bad, because there is no election in which the whole nation is one constituency. In 1945 I worked for a candidate who got a majority of forty-six, so if my work converted twenty-four people the result would have been different if I had been idle. If the Labour Party had got a majority of one in Parliament I might have come to think myself quite important; but as it was I had to content myself with the pleasure of being on the winning side.

Things would be better if people took an interest in local politics, but unfortunately few do. Nor is this surprising, since most of the important issues are decided nationally, not locally. It is to be regretted that there is so little civic pride nowadays. In the Middle Ages each city wished to be pre-eminent in the splendor of its cathedral, and we still profit by the result. In our own time, Stockholm had the same feeling about its Town Hall, which is splendid. But English large towns seem to have no such feeling.

In industry there is room for a great deal of devolution. For many years the Labour Party has advocated nationalization of railways, and most railway employees have supported the Party in this. But now a good many of them are finding that the State is, after all, not so very different from a private company. It is equally remote, and under a Conservative government it will be equally likely to be on bad terms with the unions. In fact nationalization needs to be supplemented by a measure of limited self-government for the railways, the railway government being elected democratically by the employees.

In all federal systems, the general principle should be to divide the affairs of each component body into home affairs and foreign affairs, the component bodies having free control of their home affairs, and the federal body having authority in matters which are foreign affairs for the components but not for it. It, in turn, should be a unit in a wider federation, and so on until we reach the world government, which, for the present, would have no foreign affairs. Of course it is not always easy to decide whether a matter is purely local or not, but this will be a question for the law courts, as in America and Australia.

This principle should be applied not only geographically, but also vocationally. In old days, when travel was slow and roads often impassable, geographical location was more important than it is now. Now, especially in a small country like ours, there would be no difficulty in allocating certain governmental functions to bodies like the trade unions, which classify people by their occupation, not by their habitation. The foreign relations of an industry are access to raw material, quantity and price of finished product. These it should not control. But everything else it should be free to decide for itself.

In such a system, there would be many more opportunities of individual initiative than there are at present, although central control would remain wherever it is essential. Of course the system would be difficult to work in time of war, and so long as there is imminent risk of war it is impossible to escape from the authority of the State except to a very limited degree. It is mainly war that has caused the excessive power of modern States, and until the fear of war is removed it is inevitable that everything should be subordinated to short-term efficiency. But I have thought it worth while to think for a moment of the world as it may be when a world government has ended the present nightmare dread of war.

In addition to the kind of federalism that I have been speaking of, there is, for certain purposes, a somewhat different method which can be advantageous. It is that of bodies which, though really part of the State, have a very considerable degree of independence. Such are, for example, the universities, the Royal Society, the B.B.C., and the Port of of London Authority. The smooth working of such bodies depends upon a certain degree of homogeneity in the community. If the Royal Society or the B.B.C. came to contain a majority of communists, Parliament would no doubt curtail its liberties. But in the meantime both have a good deal of autonomy, which is highly desirable. Our older universities, being governed by men with respect for learning, are, I am happy to observe, much more liberal towards academically distinguished communists than the universities of America, in which men of learning have no voice in the government.

Art and literature are peculiar in the modern world in that those who practice them retain the individual liberty of former times, and are practically untouched by scientific technique unless they are drawn into the cinema. This is more true of authors than of artists, because, as private fortunes dwindle, artists become increasingly dependent upon the patronage of public bodies. But if an artist is prepared to starve, nothing can prevent him from doing his best. However. the position of both artists and authors is precarious.

In Russia they are already mere licensed sycophants. Elsewhere, before long, with conscription of labor, no one will be allowed to practice literature or painting unless he can get twelve magistrates or ministers of religion to testify to his competence. I am not quite sure that the aesthetic taste of these worthy men will always be impeccable.

Liberty, in the old-fashioned sense, is much more important in regard to mental than to material goods. The reason is simple: that in regard to mental goods what one man possesses is not taken from other men, whereas with material goods it is otherwise. When a limited supply of (say) food has to be shared out, the obvious principle is *justice*. This does not mean exact equality: a navvy needs more food than a bedridden old man. The principle must be, in the words of the old slogan, "to each according to his needs." There is here, however, a difficulty, much emphasized by opponents of socialism; it is that of *incentive*. Under capitalism, the incentive is fear of starvation; under communism, it is the fear of drastic police punishment. Neither is quite what the democratic socialist wants. But I do not think industry can work efficiently through the mere motive of public spirit; something more personal is necessary in normal times. My own belief is that a collective profit motive can be, and should be, combined with socialism. Take, say, coal mining. The State should decide, at the beginning of each year, what prices it is prepared to pay for coal of various qualities. Methods of mining should be left to the industry. Every technical improvement would then result in more coal or less work for miners. The profit motive, in a new form, would survive, but without the old evils. By devolution, the motive could be made to operate on each mine.

In regard to mental goods, neither justice nor incentive is

important; what is important is *opportunity*. Opportunity, of course, includes remaining alive, and to this extent involves material goods. But most men of great creative power are not interested in becoming rich, so that a modest subsistence would suffice. And if these men are put to death, like Socrates, when their work is done, no harm is done to anyone. But great harm is done if, during their lifetime, their work is hampered by authority, even if the hampering takes the form of heaping honors upon them as the price of conformity. No society can be progressive without a leaven of rebels, and modern technique makes it more and more difficult to be a rebel.

The difficulties of the problem are very great. As regards science, I do not think that any complete solution is possible. You cannot work at nuclear physics in America unless you are politically orthodox; you cannot work at any science in Russia unless you are orthodox, not only in politics, but also in science, and orthodoxy in science means accepting all Stalin's uneducated prejudices. The difficulty arises from the vast expense of scientific apparatus. There is, or was, a law that when a man is sued for debt he must not be deprived of the tools of his trade, but when his tools cost many millions of pounds the situation is very different from that of the eighteenth-century handicraftsman.

I do not think that, in the present state of the world, any government can be blamed for demanding *political* orthodoxy of nuclear physicists. If Guy Fawkes had demanded gunpowder on the ground that it was one of the tools of his trade, I think James I's government would have viewed the request somewhat coldly, and this applies with even more force to the nuclear physicists of our time: governments must demand some assurance as to *who* they are going to blow up. But there is no justification whatever for demanding *scientific* orthodoxy. Fortunately, in science it is fairly easy to estimate a man's ability. It is therefore possible to act on the principle that a scientist should be given opportunity in proportion to his ability, not to his scientific orthodoxy. I think that on the whole, in Western Europe, this principle is fairly well observed. But its observance is precarious, and mightly easily cease in a time of acute scientific controversy.

In art and literature the problem is different. On the one hand, freedom is more possible, because the authorities are not asked to provide expensive apparatus. But on the other hand merit is much more difficult to estimate. The older generation of artists and writers is almost invariably mistaken as to the younger generation: the pundits almost always condemn new men who are subsequently judged to have outstanding merit. For this reason such bodies as the French Academy or the Royal Academy are useless, if not harmful. There is no conceivable method by which the community can recognize the artist until he is old and most of his work is done. The community can only give opportunity and toleration. It can hardly be expected that the community should license every man who says he means to paint, and should support him for his daubs however execrable they may be. I think the only solution is that the artist should support himself by work other than his art, until such time as he gets a knighthood. He should seek ill-paid half-time employment, live austerely, and do his creative work in his spare time. Sometimes less arduous solutions are possible: a dramatist can be an actor, a composer can be a performer. But in any case the artist or writer must, while he is young, keep his creative work outside the economic machine and make his living by work of which the value is obvious to the authorities. For if his creative work affords his official means of livelihood, it will be hampered and impaired by the ignorant censorship of the authorities. The most that can be hoped—and this is much—is that a man who does good work will not be punished for it.

The construction of Utopias used to be despised as the foolish refuge of those who could not face the real world. But in our time social change has been so rapid, and so largely inspired by utopian aspirations, that it is more necessary than it used to be to consider the wisdom or unwisdom of dominant aspirations. Marx, though he made fun of utopians, was himself one of them, and so was his disciple Lenin. Lenin had the almost unique privilege of actually constructing his Utopia in a great and powerful State; he was the nearest approach known to history to Plato's philosopher king. The fact that the result is unsatisfactory is, I think, mainly due to intellectual errors on the part of Marx and Lenin—errors which remain intellectual although they have an emotional source in the dictatorial character of the two men. Western democrats are constantly accused, even by many of their friends, of having no inspiring and coherent doctrine with which to confront communism. I think this challenge can be met. I will therefore repeat, in a less argumentative form, the conception of a good society by which I believe that democratic socialism should be guided.

In a good society, a man should (1) be useful, (2) be as far as possible secure from undeserved misfortune, (3) have opportunity for initiative in all ways not positively harmful to others. No one of these three is absolute. A lunatic cannot be useful, but should not on that account be punished. During a war, undeserved misfortunes are unavoidable. In a time of great public disaster, even the greatest artist may have to give up his own work in order to combat fire or flood or pestilence. Our three requisites are general directives, not absolute imperatives.

(1) When I say that a man should be "useful," I am thinking of him in relation to the community, and am accepting the community's judgment as to what is useful. If a man is a great poet or a Seventh-Day Adventist, he personally may think that the most useful thing he can do is to write verses or preach that the Sabbath should be observed on Saturday. But if the community does not agree with him, he should find some way of earning his living which is generally acknowledged to be useful, and confine to his leisure hours his activities as a poet or a missionary.

(2) Security has been one of the chief aims of British social legislation since the great days of Lloyd George. Unemployment, illness, and old age do not deserve punishment, and should not be allowed to bring avoidable suffering. The community has the right to exact work from those capable of work, but it has also the duty to support all those willing to work, whether in fact they are able to work or not. Security has also legal aspects: a man must not be subject to arbitrary arrest or to confiscation of his property without judicial or legislative sanction.

(3) Opportunity for initiative is a more difficult matter, but not less important. Usefulness and security form the basis of the theoretical case for socialism, but without opportunity for initiative a socialist community might have little merit. Read Plato's *Republic* and More's *Utopia*— both socialist works—and imagine yourself living in the community portrayed by either. You will see that boredom would drive you to suicide or rebellion. A man who has

never had security may think that it would satisfy him, but in fact—to borrow an analogy from mountaineering—it is only a base camp from which dangerous ascents can begin. The impulse to danger and adventure is deeply ingrained in human nature, and no society which ignores it can long be stable.

A democratic scientific society, by exacting service and conferring security, forbids or prevents much personal initiative which is possible in a less well-regulated world. Eighty years ago, Vanderbilt and Jay Gould each claimed ownership of the Erie Railroad; each had a printing press to prove how many shares he owned; each had a posse of corrupt judges ready to give any legal decision demanded of them; each had physical control of a portion of the rolling stock. On a given day, one started a train at one end of the line, the other at the other; the trains met in the middle; each was full of hired bravos, and the two gangs had a six-hour battle. Obviously Vanderbilt and Jay Gould enjoyed themselves hugely; so did the bravos; so did the whole American nation except those who wanted to use the Erie Railroad. So did I when I read about the affair. Nevertheless, the affair was thought to be a scandal. Nowadays the impulse to such delights has to seek satisfaction in the construction of hydrogen bombs, which is at once more harmful and less emotionally satisfying. If the world is ever to have peace, it must find ways of combining peace with the possibility of adventures that are not destructive.

The solution lies in providing opportunities for contests that are not conducted by violent means. This is one of the great merits of democracy. If you hate socialism or capitalism, you are not reduced to assassinating Mr. Attlee or Mr. Churchill; you can make election speeches, or, if that doesn't satisfy you, get yourself elected to Parliament. So long as the old Liberal freedoms survive, you can engage in propaganda for whatever excites you. Such activities suffice to satisfy most men's combative instincts. Creative impulses which are not combative, such as those of the artist and the writer, cannot be satisfied in this way, and for them the only solution, in a socialist State, is liberty to employ your leisure as you like. This is the only solution, because such activities are sometimes extremely valuable, but the community has no way of judging, in a given case, whether the artist's or writer's work is worthless or shows immortal genius. Such activities, therefore, must not be systematized or controlled. Some part of life—perhaps the most important part—must be left to the spontaneous action of individual impulse, for where *all* is system there will be mental and spiritual death.

CHAPTER V

Science and War

THE connection of science with war has grown gradually more and more intimate. It began with Archimedes, who helped his cousin the tyrant of Syracuse
to defend that city against the Romans in 212 B.C. In Plu-
tarch's *Life of Marcellus* there is a highly romantic and
obviously largely mythical account of the engines of war
that Archimedes invented. I quote North.

(Before war had begun)
The king prayed him to make him some engines, both to assault
and defend, in all manner of sieges and assaults. So Archimedes
made him many engines, but King Hieron never occupied any of
them, because he reigned the most part of his time in peace without
any wars. But this provision and munition of engines served the
Syracusans marvellously at that time (when Syracuse was besieged). When Archimedes fell to handle his engines, and to set
them at liberty, there flew in the air infinite kinds of shot, and
marvellous great stones, with an incredible great noise and force
on the sudden, upon the footmen that came to assault the city by
land, bearing down and tearing in pieces all those which came
against them, or in what place soever they lighted, no earthly
body being able to resist the violence of so heavy a weight: so that
all their ranks were marvellously disordered. And as for the galleys
that gave assault by sea, some were sunk with long pieces of

timber, which were suddenly blown over the walls with force of their engines into their galleys, and so sunk them by their over-great weight. Other being hoist up by their prows with hands of iron, and hooks made like cranes' bills, plunged their poops into the sea. Other being taken up with certain engines fastened within, one contrary to another, made them turn in the air like a whirligig, and so cast them upon the rocks by the tour walls, and splitted them all to fitters, to the great spoil and murder of the persons that were within them. And sometimes the ships and galleys were lift clean out of the water, that it was a fearful thing to see them hang and turn in the air as they did: until that, casting their men within them over the hatches, some here, some there, by this terrible turning, they came in the end to be empty, and to break against the walls, or else to fall into the sea again, when their engine left their hold.

In spite of all this scientific technique, however, the Romans were victorious, and Archimedes was killed by a plain infantry soldier. One can imagine the exultation of Roman Blimps at the proof that once more these newfangled devices of long-haired scientists had been defeated by the old tried traditional forces by means of which the Empire's greatness had been built up.

Nevertheless science continued to play a decisive part in war. Greek fire kept the Byzantine Empire in existence for centuries. Artillery destroyed the feudal system, and by making English archery obsolete created the myth of Joan of Arc. The greatest men of the Renaissance commended them-selves to the powerful by their skill in scientific warfare. When Leonardo wanted to get a job from the Duke of Milan, he wrote the Duke a long letter about his improve-ments in the art of fortification, and in the last sentence mentioned briefly that he could also paint a bit. He got the job, though I doubt if the Duke read as far as the last sentence. When Galileo wanted employment under the Grand Duke of Tuscany, it was on his calculations of the trajectories of cannon-balls that he relied. In the French Revolution, such men of science as were not guillotined owed their immunity to their contributions to the war effort. I know of only one instance on the other side. During the Crimean War Faraday was consulted as to the use of poison gas. He replied that it was entirely feasible, but was to be condemned on grounds of humanity. In those inefficient days his opinion prevailed. But that was long ago.

The Crimean War could still be celebrated by Kinglake in the romantic language of the ages of chivalry, but modern war is a very different matter. No doubt there are still gallant officers and brave men who die nobly in the ancient manner, but it is not they who are important. One nuclear physicist is worth more than many divisions of infantry. And apart from applications of the latest science, what secures success in war is not heroic armies but heavy industry. Consider the success of the United States after Pearl Harbor. No nation has ever shown more heroism than was shown by the Japanese, but they were defeated by American industrial productivity. It is to steel and oil and uranium, not to martial ardor, that modern nations must look for victory in war.

Modern warfare, so far, has not been more destructive of life than the warfare of less scientific ages, for the increased deadliness of weapons has been offset by the improvement in medicine and hygiene. Until recent times, pestilence almost invariably proved far more fatal than enemy action. When Sennacherib besieged Jerusalem, 185,000 of his army died in one night, "and when they arose early in the morning, behold they were all dead corpses" (II Kings xix. 35). The plague in Athens did much to decide the Peloponnesian War. The many wars between Syracuse and Carthage were usually ended by pestilence. Barbarossa, after he had completely defeated the Lombard League, lost almost his whole army by disease, and had to fly secretly over the Alps. The mortality rate in such campaigns was far greater than in the two great wars of our own century. I do not say that future wars will have as low a casualty rate as the last two; that is a matter to which I will come shortly. I say only, what many people do not realize, that up to the present science has not made war more destructive.

There are, however, other respects in which the evils of war have much increased. France was at war, almost continuously, from 1792 to 1815, and in the end suffered complete defeat, but the population of France did not, after 1815, suffer anything comparable to what has been suffered throughout Central Europe since 1945. A modern nation at war is more organized, more disciplined, and more completely concentrated on the effort to secure victory, than was possible in pre-industrial times; the consequence is that defeat is more serious, more disorganizing, more demoralizing to the general population, than it was in the days of Napoleon.

But even in this respect it is not possible to make a general rule. Some wars in the past were quite as disorganizing and as destructive of the civilization of devastated areas as was the Second World War. North Africa has never regained the level of prosperity that it enjoyed under the Romans. Persia never recovered from the Mongols nor Syria from the Turks. There have always been two kinds of wars, those in which the vanquished incurred disaster, and those in which they only incurred discomfort. We seem, unfortunately, to be entering upon an era in which wars are of the former sort.

The atom bomb, and still more the hydrogen bomb, have caused new fears, involving new doubts as to the effects of science on human life. Some eminent authorities, including Einstein, have pointed out that there is a danger of the extinction of all life on this planet. I do not myself think that this will happen in the next war, but I think it may well happen in the next but one, if that is allowed to occur. If this expectation is correct, we have to choose, within the next fifty years or so, between two alternatives. Either we must allow the human race to exterminate itself, or we must forgo certain liberties which are very dear to us, more especially the liberty to kill foreigners whenever we feel so disposed. I think it probable that mankind will choose its own extermination as the preferable alternative. The choice will be made, of course, by persuading ourselves that it is not being made, since (so militarists on both sides will say) the victory of the right is certain without risk of universal disaster. We are perhaps living in the last age of man, and, if so, it is to science that he will owe his extinction.

If, however, the human race decides to let itself go on living, it will have to make very drastic changes in its ways of thinking, feeling, and behaving. We must learn not to say: "Never! Better death than dishonor." We must learn to submit to law, even when imposed by aliens whom we hate and despise, and whom we believe to be blind to all considerations of righteousness. Consider some concrete examples. Jews and Arabs will have to agree to submit to arbitration; if the award goes against the Jews, the President of the United States will have to insure the victory of the party to which he is opposed, since, if he supports the international authority, he will lose the Jewish vote in New York State. On the other hand, if the award goes in favor of the Jews, the Mohammedan world will be indignant, and will be supported by all other malcontents. Or, to take another instance, Eire will demand the right to oppress the Protestants of Ulster, and on this issue the United States will support Eire while Britain will support Ulster. Could an international authority survive such a dissension? Again: India and Pakistan cannot agree about Kashmir, therefore one of them must support Russia and the other the United States. It will be obvious to anyone who is an interested party in one of these disputes that the issue is far more important than the continuance of life on our planet. The hope that the human race will allow itself to survive is therefore somewhat slender.

But if human life *is* to continue in spite of science, mankind will have to learn a discipline of the passions which, in the past, has not been necessary. Men will have to submit to the law, even when they think the law unjust and iniquitous. Nations which are persuaded that they are only demanding the barest justice will have to acquiesce when this demand is denied them by the neutral authority. I do not say that this is easy; I do not prophesy that it will happen; I say only that if it does not happen the human race will perish, and will perish as a result of science.

A clear choice must be made within fifty years, the choice between Reason and Death. And by "Reason" I mean willingness to submit to law as declared by an international authority. I fear that mankind may choose Death. I hope I am mistaken.

CHAPTER VI

Science and Values

THE philosophy which has seemed appropriate to science has varied from time to time. To Newton and most of his English contemporaries science seemed to afford proof of the existence of God as the Almighty Lawgiver: He had decreed the law of gravitation and whatever other natural laws had been discovered by Englishmen. In spite of Copernicus, man was still the *moral* center of the universe, and God's purposes were mainly concerned with the human race. The more radical among the French *philosophes*, being politically in conflict with the Church, took a different view. They did not admit that laws imply a lawgiver; on the other hand, they thought that physical laws could explain human behavior. This led them to materialism and denial of free will. In their view, the universe has no purpose and man is an insignificant episode. The vastness of the universe impressed them and inspired in them a new form of humility to replace that which atheism had made obsolete. This point of view is well expressed in a little poem by Leopardi and expresses, more nearly than any other known to me, my own feeling about the universe and human passions:

THE INFINITE [1]

Dear to me always was this lonely hill
And this hedge that excludes so large a part
Of the ultimate horizon from my view.
But as I sit and gaze, my thought conceives
Interminable vastnesses of space
Beyond it, and unearthly silences,
And profoundest calm; whereat my heart almost
Becomes dismayed. And as I hear the wind
Blustering through these branches, I find myself
Comparing with this sound that infinite silence;
And then I call to mind eternity,
And the ages that are dead, and this that now
Is living, and the noise of it. And so
In this immensity my thought sinks drowned:
And sweet it seems to shipwreck in this sea.

But this has become an old-fashioned way of feeling. Science used to be valued as a means of getting to *know* the world; now, owing to the triumph of technique, it is conceived as showing how to *change* the world. The new point of view, which is adopted in practice throughout America and Russia, and in theory by many modern philosophers, was first proclaimed by Marx in 1845, in his *Theses on Feuerbach*. He says:

The question whether objective truth belongs to human thinking is not a question of theory, but a practical question. The truth, i.e. the reality and power, of thought must be demonstrated in practice. The contest as to the reality or non-reality of a thought which is isolated from practice, is a purely scholastic question. . . .

[1] Translation by R. C. Trevelyan from *Translations from Leopardi*; Cambridge University Press, 1941.

Philosophers have only *interpreted* the world in various ways, but the real task is to alter it.

From the point of view of technical philosophy, this theory has been best developed by John Dewey, who is universally acknowledged as America's most eminent philosopher.

This philosophy has two aspects, one thoretical and the other ethical. On the theoretical side, it analyzes away the concept "truth," for which it substitutes "utility." It used to be thought that, if you believed Caesar crossed the Rubicon, you believed truly, because Caesar did cross the Rubicon. Not so, say the philosophers we are considering: to say that your belief is "true" is another way of saying that you will find it more profitable than the opposite belief. I might object that there have been cases of historical beliefs which, after being generally accepted for a long time, have in the end been admitted to be mistaken. In the case of such beliefs, every examinee would find the accepted falsehood of his time more profitable than the as yet unacknowledged truth. But this kind of objection is swept aside by the contention that a belief may be "true" at one time and "false" at another. In 1920 it was "true" that Trotsky had a great part in the Russian Revolution; in 1930 it was "false." The results of this view have been admirably worked out in George Orwell's "1984."

This philosophy derives its inspiration from science in several different ways. Take first its best aspect, as developed by Dewey. He points out that scientific theories change from time to time, and that what recommends a theory is that it "works." When new phenomena are discovered, for which it no longer "works," it is discarded. A theory—so Dewey concludes—is a tool like another; it enables us to manipulate raw material. Like any other tool, it is judged good or bad by its efficiency in this manipulation, and like any other tool, it is good at one time and bad at another. While it is good it may be called "true," but this word must not be allowed its usual connotations. Dewey prefers the phrase "warranted assertibility" to the word "truth."

The second source of the theory is technique. What do we want to know about electricity? Only how to make it work for us. To want to know more is to plunge into useless metaphysics. Science is to be admired because it gives us power over nature, and the power comes wholly from technique. Therefore an interpretation which reduces science to technique keeps all the useful part, and dismisses only a dead weight of medieval lumber. If technique is all that interests you, you are likely to find this argument very convincing.

The third attraction of prgamatism—which cannot be wholly separated from the second—is love of power. Most men's desires are of various kinds. There are the pleasures of sense; there are aesthetic pleasures and pleasures of contemplation; there are private affections; and there is power. In an individual, any one of these may acquire predominance over the others. If love of power dominates, you arrive at Marx's view that what is important is not to understand the world, but to change it. Traditional theories of knowledge were invented by men who loved contemplation—a monkish taste, according to modern devotees of mechanism. Mechanism augments human power to an enormous degree. It is therefore this aspect of science that attracts the lovers of power. And if power is all you want from science, the pragmatist theory gives you just what you want, without accretions that to you seem irrelevant. It gives you even more than you could have expected, for if you control the police it gives you the godlike power of *making truth*. You cannot make the sun cold, but you can confer pragmatic "truth" on the proposition "the sun is cold" if you can ensure that everyone who denies it is liquidated. I doubt whether Zeus could do more.

This engineer's philosophy, as it may be called, is distinguished from common sense and from most other philosophies by its rejection of "fact" as a fundamental concept in defining "truth." If you say, for example, "the South Pole is cold," you say something which, according to traditional views, is "true" in virtue of a "fact," namely that the South Pole is cold. And this is a fact, not because people believe it, or because it pays to believe it; it just *is* a fact. Facts, when they are not about human beings and their doings, represent the limitations of human power. We find ourselves in a universe of a certain sort, and we find out what sort of universe it is by observation, not by self-assertion. It is true that we can make changes on or near the surface of the earth, but not elsewhere. Practical men have no wish to make changes elsewhere, and can therefore accept a philosophy which treats the surface of the earth as if it were the whole universe. But even on the surface of the earth our power is limited. To forget that we are hemmed in by facts which are for the most part independent of our desires is a form of insane megalomania. This kind of insanity has grown up as a result of the triumph of scientific technique. Its latest manifestation is Stalin's refusal to believe that heredity can have the temerity to ignore Soviet decrees, which is like Xerxes whipping the Hellespont to teach Poseidon a lesson.

"The pragmatic theory of truth [I wrote in 1907] is inherently connected with the appeal to force. If there is a non-human truth, which one man may know while another does not, there is a standard outside the disputants, to which, we may urge, the dispute ought to be submitted; hence a pacific and judicial settlement of disputes is at least theoretically possible. If, on the contrary, the only way of discovering which of the disputants is in the right is to wait and see which of them is successful, there is no longer any principle except force by which the issue can be decided. . . . In international matters, owing to the fact that the disputants are often strong enough to be independent of outside control, these considerations become more important. The hopes of international peace, like the achievement of internal peace, depend upon the creation of an effective force of public opinion formed upon an estimate of the rights and wrongs of disputes. Thus it would be misleading to say that the dispute is decided by force, without adding that force is dependent upon justice. But the possibility of such a public opinion depends upon the possibility of a standard of justice which is a cause, not an effect, of the wishes of the community; and such a standard of justice seems incompatible with the pragmatist philosophy. This philosophy, therefore, although it begins with liberty and toleration, develops, by inherent necessity, into the appeal to force and the arbitrament of the big battalions. By this development it becomes equally adapted to democracy at home and to imperialism abroad. Thus here again it is more delicately adjusted to the requirements of the time than any other philosophy which has hitherto been invented.

"To sum up: Pragmatism appeals to the temper of mind which finds on the surface of this planet the whole of its imaginative material; which feels confident of progress, and unaware of non-human limitations to human power; which loves battle, with all the attendant risks, because it has no real doubt that it will achieve victory; which desires religion, as it desires railways and electric light, as a comfort and a help in the affairs of this world, not as providing non-human objects to satisfy the hunger for perfection. But for those who feel that life on this planet would be a life in prison if it were not for the windows into a greater world beyond; for those to whom a belief in man's omnipotence seems arrogant; who desire rather the stoic freedom that comes of mastery over the passions than the Napoleonic domination that sees the kingdoms of this world at its feet—in a word, to men who do not find man an adequate object of their worship, the pragmatist's world will seem narrow and petty, robbing life of all that gives it value, and making man himself smaller by depriving the universe which he contemplates of all its splendor."

Let us now try to sum up what increases in human happiness science has rendered possible, and what ancient evils it is in danger of intensifying.

I do not pretend that there is any way of arriving at the millennium. Whatever our social institutions, there will be death and illness (though in a diminishing quantity); there will be old age and insanity; there will be either danger or boredom. So long as the present family survives, there will be unrequited love and parents' tyranny and children's ingratitude; and if something new were substituted for the family, it would bring new evils, probably worse. Human life cannot be made a matter of unalloyed bliss, and to allow oneself excessive hopes is to court disappointment. Nevertheless what can be soberly hoped is very considerable. In what follows, I am not prophesying what *will* happen, but pointing out the best that *may* happen, and the further fact that this best will happen if it is widely desired.

There are two ancient evils that science, unwisely used, may intensify: they are tyranny and war. But I am concerned now rather with pleasant possibilities than with unpleasant ones.

Science can confer two kinds of benefits: it can diminish bad things, and it can increase good things. Let us begin with the former.

Science can abolish poverty and excessive hours of labor. In the earliest human communities, before agriculture, each human individual required two or more square miles to sustain life. Subsistence was precarious and death from starvation must have been frequent. At that stage, men had the same mixture of misery and carefree enjoyment as still makes up the lives of other animals.

Agriculture was a technical advance of the same kind of importance as attaches to modern machine industry. The way that agriculture was used is an awful warning to our age. It introduced slavery and serfdom, human sacrifice, absolute monarchy and large wars. Instead of raising the standard of life, except for a tiny governing minority, it merely increased the population. On the whole, it probably increased the sum of human misery. It is not impossible that industrialism may take the same course.

Fortunately, however, the growth of industrialism has coincided in the West with the growth of democracy. It is possible now, if the population of the world does not increase too fast, for one man's labor to produce much more than is needed to provide a bare subsistence for himself and his family. Given an intelligent democracy not misled by some dogmatic creed, this possibility will be used to raise the standard of life. It has been so used, to a limited extent, in Britain and America, and would have been so used more effectively but for war. Its use in raising the standard of life has depended mainly upon three things: democracy, trade unionism, and birth control. All three, of course, have incurred hostility from the rich. If these three things can be extended to the rest of the world as it becomes industrialized, and if the danger of great wars can be eliminated, poverty can be abolished throughout the whole world and excessive hours of labor will no longer be necessary anywhere. But without these three things, industrialism will create a regime like that in which the Pharaohs built the pyramids. In particular, if world population continues to increase at the present rate, the abolition of poverty and excessive work will be totally impossible.

Science has already conferred an immense boon on mankind by the growth of medicine. In the eighteenth century people expected most of their children to die before they were grown up. Improvement began at the beginning of the nineteenth century, chiefly owing to vaccination. It has continued ever since and is still continuing. In 1920 the infant mortality in England and Wales was 80 per thousand, in 1948 it was 34 per thousand. The general death rate in 1948 $(10 \cdot 8)$ was the lowest ever recorded up to that date. There is no obvious limit to the improvement of health that can be brought about by medicine. The sum of human suffering has also been much diminished by the discovery of anesthetics.

The general diminution of lawlessness and crimes of violence would not have been possible without science. If you read eighteenth-century novels, you get a strange impression of London: unlighted streets, footpads and highwaymen, nothing that we should count as a police force, but, in a futile attempt to compensate for all this, an abominably savage and ferocious criminal law. Street lighting, telephones, finger-printing, and the psychology of crime and punishment are scientific advances which have made it possible for the police to reduce crime below anything that the most utopian philosopher of the "Age of Reason" would have imagined possible.

Coming now to positive goods, there is, to begin with, an immense increase of education which has been rendered possible by the increased productivity of labor. As regards general education, this is most marked in America, where even university education is free. If I took a taxi in New York, I would often find that the driver was a Ph.D., who would start arguing about philosophy at imminent risk to himself and me. But in England as well as in America the improvement at the highest level is equally remarkable. Read, for instance, Gibbon's account of Oxford.

With this goes an increase of opportunity. It is much easier than it used to be for an able young man without what are called "natural" advantages (i.e. inherited wealth) to rise to a position in which he can make the best use of his talents. In this respect there is still much to be done, but there is every reason to expect that in England and in America it will be done. The waste of talent in former times must have been appalling; I shudder to think how many "mute inglorious Miltons" there must have been. Our modern Miltons, alas, remain for the most part inglorious, though not mute. But ours is not a poetic age.

Finally, there is more diffused happiness than ever before, and if the fear of war were removed this improvement would be very much greater than it is.

Let us consider for a moment the kind of disposition that must be widely diffused if a good world is to be created and sustained.

I will begin with the intellectual temper that is required. There must be in many a desire to know the important facts, and in most an unwillingness to give assent to pleasant illusions. There are in the world at the present day two great opposing systems of dogma: Catholicism and Communism. If you believe either with such intensity that you are prepared to face martyrdom, you can live a happy life, and even enjoy a happy death if it comes quickly. You can inspire converts, you can create an army, you can stir up hatred of the opposite dogma and its adherents, and generally you can *seem* immensely effective. I am constantly asked: What can you, with your cold rationalism, offer to the seeker after salvation that is comparable to the cozy homelike comfort of a fenced-in dogmatic creed?

To this the answer is many-sided. In the first place, I do not say that I can offer as much happiness as is to be obtained by the abdication of reason. I do not say that I can offer as much happiness as is to be obtained from drink or drugs or amassing great wealth by swindling widows and orphans. It is not the happiness of the individual convert that concerns me; it is the happiness of mankind. If you genuinely desire the happiness of mankind, certain forms of ignoble personal happiness are not open to you. If your child is ill, and you are a conscientious parent, you accept medical diagnosis, however doubtful and discouraging; if you accept the cheerful opinion of a quack and your child consequently dies, you are not excused by the pleasantness of belief in the quack while it lasted. If people loved humanity as genuinely as they love their children, they would be as unwilling in politics as in the home to let themselves be deceived by comfortable fairy tales.

The next point is that all fanatical creeds do harm. This is obvious when they have to compete with other fanaticisms, since in that case they promote hatred and strife. But it is true even when only one fanatical creed is in the field. It cannot allow free inquiry, since this might shake its hold. It must oppose intellectual progress. If, as is usually the case, it involves a priesthood, it gives great power to a caste professionally devoted to maintenance of the intellectual *status quo* and to a pretense of certainty where in fact there is no certainty.

Every fanatical creed essentially involves hatred. I knew once a fanatical advocate of an international language, but he preferred Ido to Esperanto. Listening to his conversation, I was appalled by the depravity of the Esperantists, who, it seemed, had sunk to hitherto unimaginable depths of wickedness. Luckily, my friend failed to convince any government, and so the Esperantists survived. But if he had been at the head of a State of two hundred million inhabitants, I shudder to think what would have happened to them.

Very often the element of hatred in a fanatical doctrine becomes predominant. People who tell you they love the proletariat often in fact only hate the rich. Some people who believe that you should love your neighbor as yourself think it right to hate those who do not do so. As these are the vast majority, no notable increase of loving-kindness results from their creed.

Apart from such specific evils, the whole attitude of accepting a belief unquestioningly on a basis of authority is contrary to the scientific spirit, and, if widespread, scarcely compatible with the progress of science. Not only the Bible, but even the works of Marx and Engels, contain demonstrably false statements. The Bible says the hare chews the cud, and Engels said that the Austrians would win the war of

1866. These are only arguments against fundamentalists. But when a Sacred Book is retained while fundamentalism is rejected, the authority of The Book becomes vested in the priesthood. The meaning of "dialectical materialism" changes every decade, and the penalty for a belated interpretation is death or the concentration camp.

The triumphs of science are due to the substitution of observation and inference for authority. Every attempt to revive authority in intellectual matters is a retrograde step. And it is part of the scientific attitude that the pronouncements of science do not claim to be certain, but only to be the most probable on present evidence. One of the greatest benefits that science confers upon those who understand its spirit is that it enables them to live without the delusive support of subjective certainty. That is why science cannot favor persecution.

The desire for a fanatical creed is one of the great evils of our time. There have been other ages with the same disease: the late Roman Empire and the sixteenth century are the most obvious examples. When Rome began to decay, and when, in the third century, barbarian irruptions produced fear and impoverishment, men began to look for safety in another world. Plotinus found it in Plato's eternal world, the followers of Mithra in a solar paradise, and the Christians in heaven. The Christians won, largely because their dogmatic certainty was the greatest. Having won, they started persecuting each other for small deviations, and hardly had leisure to notice the barbarian invaders except to observe that they were Arians—the ancient equivalent of Trotskyites. The religious fervor of that time was a product of fear and despair; so is the religious fervor—Christian or communist— of our age. It is an irrational reaction to danger, tending to bring about what it fears. Dread of the hydrogen bomb promotes fanaticism, and fanaticism is more likely than anything else to lead to actual use of the hydrogen bomb. Heavenly salvation perhaps, if the fanatics are right, but earthly salvation is not to be found along that road.

I will say a few words about the connection of love with intellectual honesty. There are several different attitudes that may be adopted towards the spectacle of intolerable suffering. If you are a sadist, you may find pleasure in it; if you are completely detached, you may ignore it; if you are a sentimentalist, you may persuade yourself that it is not as bad as it seems; but if you feel genuine compassion you will try to apprehend the evil truly in order to be able to cure it. The sentimentalist will say that you are coldly intellectual, and that, if you really minded the sufferings of others, you could not be so scientific about them. The sentimentalist will claim to have a tenderer heart than yours, and will show it by letting the suffering continue rather than suffer himself.

There is a tender hearted lady in Gilbert and Sullivan who remarks:

> I heard one day The fatal steel
> A gentleman say But come in twain
> That criminals who Without much pain.
> Are sawn in two If this be true
> Do not much feel How lucky for you.

Similarly, the men who made the Munich surrender would pretend, (*a*) that the Nazis didn't go in for pogroms, (*b*) that Jews enjoyed being massacred. And fellow-travelers maintain, (*a*) that there is no forced labor in Russia, (*b*) that there is nothing Russians find more delectable than being worked to death in an arctic winter. Such men are not "coldly intellectual."

The most disquiting psychological feature of our time, and the one which affords the best argument for the necessity of some creed, however irrational, is the death wish. Everyone knows how some primitive communities, brought suddenly into contact with white men, become listless, and finally die from mere absence of the will to live. In Western Europe, the new conditions of danger which exist are having something of the same effect. Facing facts is painful, and the way out is not clear. Nostalgia takes the place of energy directed towards the future. There is a tendency to shrug the shoulders and say, "Oh well, if we are exterminated by hydrogen bombs, it will save a lot of trouble." This is a tired and feeble reaction, like that of the late Romans to the barbarians. It can only be met by courage, hope, and a reasoned optimism. Let us see what basis there is for hope.

First: I have no doubt that, leaving on one side, for the moment, the danger of war, the average level of happiness, in Britain as well as in America, is higher than in any previous community at any time. Moreover improvement continues whenever there is not war. We have therefore something important to conserve.

There are certain things that our age needs, and certain things that it should avoid. It needs compassion and a wish that mankind should be happy; it needs the desire for knowledge and the determination to eschew pleasant myths; it needs, above all, courageous hope and the impulse to creativeness. The things that it must avoid, and that have brought it to the brink of catastrophe, are cruelty, envy, greed, competitiveness, search for irrational subjective certainty, and what Freudians call the death wish.

The root of the matter is a very simple and old-fashioned thing, a thing so simple that I am almost ashamed to mention it, for fear of the derisive smile with which wise cynics will greet my words. The thing I mean—please forgive me for mentioning it— is love, Christian love, or compassion. If you feel this, you have a motive for existence, a guide in action, a reason for courage, an imperative necessity for intellectual honesty. If you feel this, you have all that anybody should need in the way of religion. Although you may not find happiness, you will never know the deep despair of those whose life is aimless and void of purpose; for there is always something that you can do to diminish the awful sum of human misery.

What I do want to stress is that the kind of lethargic despair which is now not uncommon, is irrational. Mankind is in the position of a man climbing a difficult and dangerous precipice, at the summit of which there is a plateau of delicious mountain meadows. With every step that he climbs, his fall, if he does fall, becomes more terrible; with every step his weariness increases and the ascent grows more difficult. At last there is only one more step to be taken, but the climber does not know this, because he cannot see beyond the jutting rocks at his head. His exhaustion is so complete that he wants nothing but rest. If he lets go he will find rest in death. Hope calls: "One more effort—perhaps it will be the last effort needed." Irony retorts: "Silly fellow! Haven't you been listening to hope all this time, and see where it has landed you." Optimism says: "While there is life there is hope." Pessimism growls: "While there is life there is pain." Does the exhausted climber make one more effort, or does he let himself sink into the abyss? In a few years those of us who are still alive will know the answer.

Dropping metaphor, the present situation is as follows: Science offers the possibility of far greater well-being for the human race than has ever been known before. It offers this on certain conditions: abolition of war, even distribution of ultimate power, and limitation of the growth of population. All these are much nearer to being possible than they ever were before. In Western industrial countries, the growth of population is almost nil; the same causes will have the same effect in other countries as they become modernized, unless dictators and missionaries interfere. The even distribution of ultimate power, economic as well as political, has been nearly achieved in Britain, and other democratic countries are rapidly moving towards it. The prevention of war? It may seem a paradox to say that we are nearer to achieving this than ever before, but I am persuaded that it is true. I will explain why I think so.

In the past, there were many sovereign States, any two of which might at any moment quarrel. Attempts on the lines of the League of Nations were bound to fail, because, when a dispute arose, the disputants were too proud to accept outside arbitration, and the neutrals were too lazy to enforce it. Now there are only two sovereign States: Russia (with satellites) and the United States (with satellites). If either becomes preponderant, either by victory in war or by an obvious military superiority, the preponderant Power can establish a single Authority over the whole world, and thus make future wars impossible. At first this Authority will, in certain regions, be based on force, but if the Western nations are in control, force will as soon as possible give way to consent. When that has been achieved, the most difficult of world problems will have been solved, and science can become wholly beneficent.

I do not think there is reason to fear that such a regime, once established, would be unstable. The chief causes of large-scale violence are: love of power, competition, hate and fear. Love of power will have no national outlet when all serious military force is concentrated in the international army. Competition will be effectively regulated by law, and mitigated by governmental controls. Fear—in the acute form in which we know it—will disappear when war is no longer to be expected. There remains hate and malevolence. This has a deep hold on human nature. We all believe at once any gossip discreditable to our neighbors, however slender the evidence may be. After the First World War many people hated Germany so much that they could not believe in injury to themselves as a necessary result of extreme severity to the Germans. One sees in Congress a widespread reluctance to admit that self-preservation requires help to Western Europe. America wishes to sell without buying, but finds that this often involves giving rather than selling; the benefit to the recipients is felt by many to be almost unendurable. This wide diffusion of malevolence is one of the most unfortunate things in human nature, and it must be lessened if a world State is to be stable.

I am persuaded that it can be lessened, and very quickly. If peace becomes secure there will be a very rapid increase of material prosperity, and this tends more than anything else to provide a mood of kindly feeling. Consider the immense diminution of cruelty in Britain during the Victorian Age; this was mainly due to rapidly increasing wealth in all classes. I think we may confidently expect a similar effect throughout the world owing to the increased wealth that will result from the elimination of war. A great deal, also, is to be hoped from a change in propaganda. Nationalist propaganda, in any violent form, will have to be illegal, and children in schools will not be taught to hate and despise foreign nations. Active instruction in the evils of the old times and the advantages of the new system would do the rest. I am convinced that only a few psychopaths would wish to return to the daily dread of radioactive disintegration.

What stands in the way? Not physical or technical obstacles, but only the evil passions in human minds: suspicion, fear, lust for power, hatred, intolerance. I will not deny that these evil passions are more dominant in the East than in the West, but they certainly exist in the West as well. The human race could, here and now, begin a rapid approach to a vastly better world, given one single condition: the removal of mutual distrust between East and West. I do not know what can be done to fulfill this condition. Most of the suggestions that I have seen have struck me as silly. Meanwhile the only thing to do is to prevent an explosion somehow, and to hope that time may bring wisdom. The near future must either be much better or much worse than the past; which it is to be will be decided within the next few years.

CHAPTER VII

Can a Scientific Society

Be Stable?[1]

IN THIS final chapter I wish to consider a purely scientific question, namely: Can a society in which thought and technique are scientific persist for a long period, as, for example, ancient Egypt persisted, or does it necessarily contain within itself forces which must bring either decay or explosion?

I will begin with some explanation of the question with which I am concerned. I call a society "scientific" in the degree to which scientific knowledge, and technique based upon that knowledge, affects its daily life, its economics, and its political organization. This, of course, is a matter of degree. Science in its early stages had few social effects except upon the small number of learned men who took an interest in it, but in recent times it has been transforming ordinary life with ever-increasing velocity.

I am using the word "stable" as it is used in physics. A top is "stable" so long as it rotates with more than a certain

---

[1] This chapter was first delivered as the Lloyd Roberts Lecture given at the Royal Society of Medicine, London, on November 29, 1949.

speed; then it becomes unstable and the top falls over. An atom which is not radioactive is "stable" until a nuclear physicist gets hold of it. A star is "stable" for millions of years, and then one day it explodes. It is in this sense that I wish to ask whether the kind of society that we are creating is "stable."

I want to emphasize that the question I am asking is purely factual. I am not considering whether it is better to be stable or to be unstable; that is a question of values, and lies outside the scope of scientific discussion. I am asking whether, in fact, it is probable or improbable that society will persist in being scientific. If it does, it must almost inevitably grow progressively more and more scientific, since new knowledge will accumulate. If it does not, there may be either a gradual decay, like the cooling of the sun by radiation, or a violent transformation, like those that cause novae to appear in the heavens. The former would show itself in exhaustion, the latter in revolution or unsuccessful war.

The problem is extremely speculative, as appears when we consider the time scale. Astronomers tell us that in all likelihood the earth will remain habitable for very many millions of years. Man has existed for about a million years. Therefore if all goes well his future should be immeasurably longer than his past.

Broadly speaking, we are in the middle of a race between human skill as to means and human folly as to ends. Given sufficient folly as to ends, every increase in the skill required to achieve them is to the bad. The human race has survived hitherto owing to ignorance and imcompetence; but, given knowledge and competence combined with folly, there can be no certainty of survival. Knowledge is power, but it is power for evil just as much as for good. It follows that, unless men increase in wisdom as much as in knowledge, increase of knowledge will be increase of sorrow.

CAUSES OF INSTABILITY

Possible causes of instability may be grouped under three heads: physical, biological, and psychological. I will begin with the physical causes.

PHYSICAL

Both industry and agriculture, to a continually increasing degree, are carried on in ways that waste the world's capital of natural resources. In agriculture this has always been the case since man first tilled the soil, except in places like the Nile Valley, where there were very exceptional conditions. While population was sparse, people merely moved on when their former fields became unsatisfactory. Then it was found that corpses could be used as fertilizers, and human sacrifice became common. This had the double advantage of increasing the yield and diminishing the number of mouths to be fed; nevertheless the method came to be frowned upon, and its place was taken by war. Wars, however, were not sufficiently destructive of human life to prevent the survivors from suffering, and the exhaustion of the soil has continued at a constantly increasing rate right down to our own day. At last the creation of the Dust Bowl in the United States compelled attention to the problem. It is now known what must be done if the world's supply of food is not to diminish catastrophically. But whether what is necessary will be done is a very doubtful question. The demand for food is so insistent, and the immediate profit so great, that only a strong and intelligent government can enforce the required measures; and in many parts of the world governments are not both strong and intelligent. I am for the present ignoring the population problem, which I shall consider presently.

Raw materials, in the long run, present just as grave a problem as agriculture. Cornwall produced tin from Phoenician times until very lately; now the tin of Cornwall is exhausted. Lightheartedly, the world contents itself with observing that there is tin in Malaya, forgetting that that too will be used up presently. Sooner or later all easily accessible tin will have been used up, and the same is true of most raw materials. The most pressing, at the moment, is oil. Without oil a nation cannot, with our present techniques, prosper industrially or defend itself in war. The supply is being rapidly depleted, and will be used up even more swiftly in the wars that are to be expected for possession of such supplies as will remain. Of course I shall be told that atomic energy will replace oil as a source of power. But what will happen when all the available uranium and thorium have done their work of killing men and fishes?

The indisputable fact is that industry—and agriculture in so far as it uses artificial fertilizers—depends upon irreplaceable materials and sources of energy. No doubt science will discover new sources as the need arises, but this will involve a gradual decrease in the yield of a given amount of land and labor, and in any case is an essentially temporary expedient. The world has been living on capital, and so long as it remains industrial it must continue to do so. This is one inescapable though perhaps rather distant source of instability in a scientific society.

BIOLOGICAL

I come now to the biological aspects of our question. If we estimate the biological success of a species by its numbers it must be admitted that man has been most remarkably successful. In his early days man must have been a very rare species. His two great advantages—the capacity of using his hands to manipulate tools, and the power of transmitting experience and invention by means of language—are slowly cumulative: at first there were few tools and there was little knowledge to transmit; moreover, no one knows at what stage language developed. However that may be, there were three great advances by means of which the human population of the globe was increased. The first was the taming of the animals that became domestic; the second was the adoption of agriculture; and the third was the industrial revolution. By means of these three advances men have become enormously more numerous than any species of large wild animals. Sheep and cattle owe their large numbers to human care; as competitors with man large mammals have no chance, as appears from the virtual extinction of the buffalo.

It is with trepidation that I advance my next thesis, which is this. Medicine cannot, except over a short period, increase the population of the world. No doubt if medicine in the fourteenth century had known how to combat the Black Death the population of Europe in the latter half of the fourteenth century would have been larger than it was. But the deficiency was soon made up to its Malthusian level by natural increase. In China, European and American medical missions do much to diminish the infant death rate; the consequence is that more children die painfully of famine at the age of five or six. The benefit to mankind is very questionable. Except where the birth rate is low the population in the long run depends upon the food supply and upon nothing else. In the Western world the fall in the birth rate has for the time being falsified Malthus's doctrine. But until lately this doctrine was true throughout the world, and it is still true in the densely populated countries of the East.

What has science done to increase population? In the first place, by machinery, fertilizers, and improved breeds it has increased the yield per acre and the yield per man-hour of labor. This is a direct effect. But there is another which is perhaps more important, at least for the moment. By improvement in means of transport it has become possible for one region to produce an excess of food while another produces an excess of industrial products or raw materials. This makes it possible—as for instance in our own country— for a region to contain a larger population than its own food resources could support. Assuming free mobility of persons and goods, it is only necessary that the whole world should produce enough food for the population of the whole world, provided the regions of deficient food production have something to offer which the regions of surplus food production are willing to accept in exchange for food. But this condition is apt to fail in bad times. In Russia, after the First World War, the peasants had just about the amount of food they wanted for themselves, and would not willingly part with any of it for the purchase of urban products. At that time, and again during the famine in the early thirties, the urban population was kept alive only by the energetic use of armed force. In the famine, as a result of government action, millions of peasants died of starvation; if the government had been neutral the town-dwellers would have died.

Such considerations point to a conclusion which, it seems to me, is too often ignored. Industry, except in so far as it ministers directly to the needs of agriculture, is a luxury: in bad times its products will be unsalable, and only force directed against food-producers can keep industrial workers alive, and that only if very many food-producers are left to die. If bad times become common, it must be inferred that industry will dwindle and that the industrialization characteristic of the last 150 years will be rudely checked.

But bad times, you may say, are exceptional, and can be dealt with by exceptional methods. This has been more or less true during the honeymoon period of industrialism, but it will not remain true unless the increase of population can be enormously diminished. At present the population of the world is increasing at about 58,000 *per diem*. War, so far, has had no very great effect on this increase, which continued throughout each of the world wars. Until the last quarter of the nineteenth century this increase was more rapid in advance countries than in backward ones, but now it is almost wholly confined to very poor countries. Of these, China and India are numerically the most important, while Russia is the most important in world politics. But I want, for the present, to confine myself, so far as I can, to biological considerations, leaving world politics on one side.

What is the inevitable result if the increase of population is not checked? There must be a very general lowering of the standard of life in what are now prosperous countries. With that lowering there must go a great diminution in the demand for industrial products. Detroit will have to give up making private cars, and confine itself to lorries. Such things as books, pianos, watches will become the rare luxuries of a few exceptionally powerful men—notably those who control the army and the police. In the end there will be a uniformity of misery, and the Malthusian law will reign unchecked. The world having been technically unified, population will increase when world harvests are good, and diminish by starvation whenever they are bad. Most of the present urban and industrial centers will have become derelict, and their inhabitants, if still alive, will have reverted to the peasant hardships of their medieval ancestors. The world will have achieved a new stability, but at the cost of everything that gives value to human life.

Are mere numbers so important that, for their sake, we should patiently permit such a state of affairs to come about? Surely not. What, then, can we do? Apart from certain deep-seated prejudices, the answer would be obvious. The nations which at present increase rapidly should be encouraged to adopt the methods by which, in the West, the increase of population has been checked. Educational propaganda, with government help, could achieve this result in a generation. There are, however, two powerful forces opposed to such a policy: one is religion, the other is nationalism. I think it is the duty of all who are capable of facing facts to realize, and to proclaim, that opposition to the spread of birth control, if successful, must inflict upon mankind the most appalling depth of misery and degradation, and that within another fifty years or so.

I do not pretend that birth control is the only way in which population can be kept from increasing. There are others, which, one must suppose, opponents of birth control would prefer. War, as I remarked a moment ago, has hitherto been disappointing in this respect, but perhaps bacteriological war may prove more effective. If a Black Death could be spread throughout the world once in every generation survivors could procreate freely without making the world too full. There would be nothing in this to offend the consciences of the devout or to restrain the ambitions of nationalists. The state of affairs might be somewhat unpleasant, but what of that? Really high-minded people are indifferent to happiness, especially other people's. However, I am wandering from the question of stability, to which I must return.

There are three ways of securing a society that shall be stable as regards population. The first is that of birth control, the second that of infanticide or really destructive wars, and the third that of general misery except for a powerful minority. All these methods have been practiced: the first, for example, by the Australian aborigines; the second by the Aztecs, the Spartans, and the rulers of Plato's *Republic;* the third in the world as some Western internationalists hope to make it and in Soviet Russia. (It is not to be supposed that Indians and Chinese like starving, but they have to endure it because the armaments of the West are too strong for them.) Of these three, only birth control avoids extreme cruelty and unhappiness for the majority of human beings. Meanwhile, so long as there is not a single world government there will be competition for power among the different nations. And as increase of population brings the threat of famine, national power will become more and more obviously the only way of avoiding starvation. There will therefore be blocs in which the hungry nations band together against those that are well fed. That is the explanation of the victory of communism in China.

These considerations prove that a scientific world society cannot be stable unless there is a world government.

It may be said, however, that this is a hasty conclusion. All that follows directly from what has been said is that, unless there is a world government which secures universal birth control, there must from time to time be great wars, in which the penalty of defeat is widespread death by starvation. That is exactly the present state of the world, and some may hold that there is no reason why it should not continue for centuries. I do not myself believe that this is possible. The two great wars that we have experienced have lowered the level of civilization in many parts of the world, and the next is pretty sure to achieve much more in this direction. Unless, at some stage, one power or group of powers emerges victorious and proceeds to establish a single government of the world with a monopoly of armed force, it is clear that the level of civilization must continually decline until scientific warfare becomes impossible—that is until science is extinct. Reduced once more to bows and arrows, Homo sapiens might breathe again, and climb anew the dreary road to a similar futile culmination.

The need for a world government, if the population problem is to be solved in any humane manner, is completely evident on Darwinian principles. Given two groups, of which one has an increasing and the other a stationary population, the one with the increasing population will (other things being equal) in time become the stronger. After victory, it will cut down the food supply of the vanquished, of whom many will die.[1] Therefore there will be a continually renewed victory of those nations that, from a world point of view, are unduly prolific. This is merely the modern form of the old struggle for existence. And given scientific powers of destruction, a world which allows this struggle to continue cannot be stable.

PSYCHOLOGICAL

The psychological conditions of stability in a scientific society are to my mind quite as important as the physical and

[1] Some may think this statement unduly brutal. But if they will look up newspapers of 1946 they will find, side by side, indignant letters saying that British labor could not be efficient on a diet of 2,500 calories, and that it was preposterous to suppose that a German needed more than 1,200 calories.

biological conditions, but they are much more difficult to discuss, because psychology is a less advanced science than either physics or biology. Nevertheless, let us make the attempt.

The old rationalist psychology used to assume that if you showed a man quite clearly that a certain course of action would lead to disaster for himself he would probably avoid it. It also took for granted a will to live, except in a negligible minority. Chiefly as a result of psychoanalysis this Benthamite belief that most men pursue their own interest in a more or less reasonable way has not now the hold on informed opinion that it formerly had. But not very many people, among those concerned with politics, have applied modern psychology to the explanation of large-scale social phenomena. This is what I propose, with much diffidence, to attempt.

Consider, as the most important illustration, the present drift towards a third world war. You are arguing, let us say, with an ordinary cheerful nonpolitical and legally sane person. You point out to him what can be done by atom bombs, what Russian occupation of Western Europe would mean in suffering and destruction of culture, what poverty and what regimentation would result even in the event of a fairly quick victory. All this he fully admits, but nevertheless you do not achieve the result for which you had hoped. You make his flesh creep, but he rather enjoys the sensation. You point out the disorganization to be expected, and he thinks: "Well, anyhow, I shan't have to go to the office every morning." You expatiate on the large number of civilian deaths that will take place, and while in the top layer of his mind, he is duly horrified, there is a whisper in a deeper layer: "Perhaps I shall become a widower, and that might not be so bad." And so, to your disgust, he takes refuge in archaic heroism, and exclaims:

> Blow wind! come wrack!
> At least we'll die with harness on our back

or whatever more prosaic equivalent he may prefer.

Psychologically, there are two opposite maladies which have become so common as to be dominant factors in politics. One is rage, the other listlessness. The typical example of the former was the mentality of the Nazis; of the latter, the mentality in France which weakened resistance to Germany before and during the war. In less acute forms these two maladies exist in other countries, and are, I think, intimately bound up with the regimentation which is associated with industrialism. Rage causes nations to embark on enterprises that are practically certain to be injurious to themselves; listlessness causes nations to be careless in warding off evils, and generally disinclined to undertake anything arduous. Both are the outcome of a deep malaise resulting from lack of harmony between disposition and mode of life.

One cause of this malaise is the rapidity of change in material conditions. Savages suddenly subjected to European restraints not infrequently die from inability to endure a life so different from what they have been accustomed to. When I was in Japan in 1921 I seemed to sense in the people with whom I talked, and in the faces of the people I met in the streets, a great nervous strain, of the sort likely to promote hysteria. I thought this came from the fact that deep-rooted unconscious expectations were adapted to old Japan, whereas the whole conscious life of town-dwellers was devoted to an effort to become as like Americans as possible. Such a malad-justment between the conscious and the unconscious was bound to produce discouragement or fury, according as the person concerned was less or more energetic. The same sort of thing happens wherever there is rapid industrialization; it must have happened with considerable intensity in Russia.

But even in a country like our own, where industrialism is old, changes occur with a rapidity which is psychologically difficult. Consider what has happened during my lifetime. When I was a child telephones were new and very rare. During my first visit to America I did not see a single motorcar. I was thirty-nine when I first saw an airplane. Broadcasting and the cinema have made the life of the young profoundly different from what it was during my own youth. As for public life, when I first became politically conscious Gladstone and Disraeli still confronted each other amid Victorian solidities, the British Empire seemed eternal, a threat to British naval supremacy was unthinkable, the country was aristocratic and rich and growing richer, and socialism was regarded as the fad of a few disgruntled and disreputable foreigners.

For an old man, with such a background, it is difficult to feel at home in a world of atomic bombs, communism, and American supremacy. Experience, formerly a help in the acquisition of political sagacity, is now a positive hindrance, because it was acquired in such different conditions. It is now scarcely possible for a man to acquire slowly the sort of wisdom which in former times caused "elders" to be respected, because the lessons of experience become out of date as fast as they are learned. Science, while it has enormously accelerated outward change, has not yet found any way of hastening psychological change, especially where the unconscious and subconscious are concerned. Few men's unconscious feels at home except in conditions very similar to those which prevailed when they were children.

Rapidity of change, however, is only one of the causes of psychological discontent. Another, perhaps more potent, is the increasing subordination of individuals to organizations, which, so far, has seemed to be an unavoidable feature of a scientific society. In a factory containing expensive plant, and depending upon the closely co-ordinated labor of many people, individual impulses must be completely controlled except by the men constituting the management. There is no possibility, in working hours, of either adventure or idleness. And even outside working hours the opportunities are few for most people. Getting from home to work and from work to home takes time; at the end of the day there is neither time nor money for anything very exciting. And what is true of workers in a factory is true, in a greater or less degree, of most people in a well-organized modern community. Most people, when they are no longer quite young, find themselves in a groove—like the man in the limerick, "not a bus, not a bus, but a tram." Energetic people become rebellious, quiet people become apathetic. War, if it comes, offers an escape. I should like a Gallup poll on the question: "Are you more or less happy now than during the war?" This question should be addressed to both men and women. I think it would be found that a very considerable percentage are less happy now than then.

This state of affairs presents a psychological problem which is too little considered by statesmen. It is hopeless to construct schemes for preserving peace if most people would rather not preserve it. As they do not admit, and perhaps do not know, that they would prefer war, their unconscious

will lead them to prefer specious schemes that are not likely
to achieve their ostensible purpose.

The difficulty of the problem arises from the highly
organic character of modern communities, which makes each
dependent upon all to a far greater degree than in pre-industrial times. This makes it necessary to restrain impulse more
than was formerly necessary. But restraint of impulse, beyond a point, is very dangerous: it causes destructiveness,
cruelty, and anarchic rebellion. Therefore, if populations are
not to rise up in a fury and destroy their own creations,
ways must be found of giving more scope for individuality
than exists for most people in the modern world. A society is
not stable unless it is on the whole satisfactory to the holders
of power and the holders of power are not exposed to the
risk of successful revolution. But it is also not stable if the
holders of power embark upon rash adventures, such as those
of the Kaiser and Hitler. These are the Scylla and Charybdis
of the psychological problem, and to steer between them is
not easy. Adventure, yes; but not adventure inspired by
destructive passions.

CONCLUSIONS

Let us now bring together the conclusions which result
from our inquiry into the various kinds of conditions that a
scientific society must fulfill if it is to be stable.

First, as regards physical conditions. Soil and raw materials
must not be used up so fast that scientific progress cannot
continually make good the loss by means of new inventions
and discoveries. Scientific progress is therefore a condition,
not merely of social progress, but even of maintaining the
degree of prosperity already achieved. Given a stationary
technique, the raw materials that it requires will be used up

in no very long time. If raw materials are not to be used up too fast, there must not be free competition for their acquisition and use but an international authority to ration them in such quantities as may from time to time seem compatible with continued industrial prosperity. And similar considerations apply to soil conservation.

Second, as regards population. If there is not to be a permanent and increasing shortage of food, agriculture must be conducted by methods which are not wasteful of soil, and increase of population must not outrun the increase in food production rendered possible by technical improvements. At present neither condition is fulfilled. The population of the world is increasing, and its capacity for food production is diminishing. Such a state of affairs obviously cannot continue very long without producing a cataclysm.

To deal with this problem it will be necessary to find ways of preventing an increase in world population. If this is to be done otherwise than by wars, pestilences, and famines, it will demand a powerful international authority. This authority should deal out the world's food to the various nations in proportion to their population at the time of the establishment of the authority. If any nation subsequently increased its population it should not on that account receive any more food. The motive for not increasing population would therefore be very compelling. What method of preventing an increase might be preferred should be left to each State to decide.

But although this is the logical solution of the problem, it is obviously at present totally impracticable. It is quite hard enough to create a strong international authority, and it will become impossible if it is to have such unpopular duties. There are, in fact, two opposite difficulties. If at the present moment the world's food were rationed evenly the Western nations would suffer what to them would seem starvation. But, on the other hand, the poorer nations are those whose population increases fastest, and who would suffer most from an allocation which was to remain constant. Therefore, as things stand, all the world would oppose the logical solution.

Taking a long view, however, it is by no means impossible that the population problem will in time solve itself. Prosperous industrial countries have low birth rates; Western nations barely maintain their numbers. If the East were to become as prosperous and as industrial as the West, the increase of population might become sufficiently slow to present no insoluble problem. At present Russia, China, and India are the three great reservoirs of procreation and poverty. If those countries reached the level of diffused well-being now existing in America their surplus population might cease to be a menace to the world.

In general terms, we may say that so far as the population problem is concerned a scientific society could be stable if all the world were as prosperous as America is now. The difficulty, however, is to reach this economic paradise without a previous success in limiting population. It cannot be done as things are now without an appalling upheaval. Only government propaganda on a large scale could quickly change the biological habits of Asia. But most Eastern governments would never consent to this except after defeat in war. And without such a change of biological habits Asia cannot become prosperous except by defeating the Western nations, exterminating a large part of their population, and opening the territories now occupied by them to Asiatic immigration. For the Western nations this is not an attractive prospect, but it is not impossible that it may happen. Irrational passions and convictions are so deeply involved in the problem that only an infinitesimal minority, even among highly educated people, are willing even to attempt to consider it rationally. That is the main reason for a gloomy prognosis.

Coming, finally, to the psychological conditions of stability, we find again that a high level of economic prosperity is essential. This would make it possible to give long holidays with full pay. In the days before currency restrictions dons and public schoolmasters used to make their lives endurable by risking death in the Alps. Given secure peace, a not excessive population, and a scientific technique of production, there is no reason why such pleasures should not be open to everybody. There will be need also of devolution, of a great extension of federal forms of government, and of keeping alive the kind of semi-independence that now exists in English universities. But I will not develop this theme, as I have dealt with it in my Reith lectures on "Authority and the Individual."

My conclusion is that a scientific society can be stable given certain conditions. The first of these is a single government of the whole world, possessing a monopoly of armed force and therefore able to enforce peace. The second condition is a general diffusion of prosperity, so that there is no occasion for envy of one part of the world by another. The third condition (which supposes the second fulfilled) is a low birth rate everywhere, so that the population of the world becomes stationary, or nearly so. The fourth condition is the provision for individual initiative both in work and in play, and the greatest diffusion of power compatible with maintaining the necessary political and economic framework.

The world is a long way from realizing these conditions, and therefore we must expect vast upheavals and appalling suffering before stability is attained. But, while upheavals and suffering have hitherto been the lot of man, we can now see, however dimly and uncertainly, a possible future culmination in which poverty and war will have been overcome, and fear, where it survives, will have become pathological. The road, I fear, is long, but that is no reason for losing sight of the ultimate hope.

ABOUT THE AUTHOR

BERTRAND ARTHUR WILLIAM RUSSELL *received the Nobel Prize for literature in 1950. He is the grandson of Lord John Russell, the British Foreign Secretary during the Civil War. Before going to Cambridge he was educated at home by governesses and tutors, acquiring a thorough knowledge of German and French; and it has been said that his "admirable and lucid English style may be attributed to the fact that he did not undergo a classical education at a public school." Certainly, this style is perceptible in the many books that have flowed from his pen during half a century—books that have shown him to be the most profound of mathematicians, the most brilliant of philosophers, and the most lucid of popularizers. His most recent major works are* A History of Western Philosophy, *published in 1945;* Human Knowledge: Its Scope and Limits, *published in 1948;* Authority and the Individual, *published in 1949;* Unpopular Essays, *that grossly mistitled book, published in 1951; and* New Hopes for a Changing World, *published in 1952.*